ISBN 0-85342-517-5

Theology Today

GENERAL EDITOR:

EDWARD YARNOLD, S. J.

No. 14

The Word Became Flesh

BY

FRANCIS J. MOLONEY

distributed by
CLERGY BOOK SERVICE
BUTLER, WISCONSIN

ACKNOWLEDGEMENTS

Thanks are due to the publishers for permission to print quotations from the following works: C. K. Barrett, *The Gospel according to St John* (S.P.C.K.); C. H. Dodd, *The Interpretation of the Fourth Gospel* (Cambridge University Press); E. C. Hoskyns and N. Davey, *The Fourth Gospel* (Faber and Faber).

ABBREVIATION

TDNT   *Theological Dictionary of the New Testament* (W. B. Eerdmans, Grand Rapids, Michigan, 1964-), the English translation of G. Kittel's *Theologisches Worterbuch zum Neuen Testament.*

CONTENTS

PREFACE

It is well known that the Gospel of St John contains a much more explicit account of the divinity of Christ than the other three. At the climax of the Gospel, the explicit confession of Jesus' divinity is put into the mouth of Thomas: 'My Lord and my God!' (20.28). However, we do not have to wait until this Easter incident before the author lets us see the nature of Jesus. He expresses his faith in particular by four titles which he applies to Jesus: the Word, the Son of God, the Son of Man and the Messiah (the Christ).

The investigation of these titles forms the major part of Father Moloney's book, together with a study of the implications of the allusions in the Gospel to Jesus' 'hour'.

Father Moloney has studied and written much about the Fourth Gospel. In this scholarly but easily intelligible book he makes available to the ordinary reader many of the ideas that he has discussed more technically elsewhere.

E. J. Yarnold, S.J.

INTRODUCTION

Some forty years ago, Charles Harold Dodd could claim, in his inaugural lecture at Cambridge, that the Fourth Gospel constituted the most acute and pressing problem in New Testament Studies.[1] Since that time scholarship has devoted a great deal of attention to the many questions associated with this unique piece of literature,[2] yet, strange as it may seem, it is still difficult to find a work in English which presents the Jesus of the Fourth Gospel.[3]

The pages which follow are an attempt to trace John's portrait of Jesus. We have approached the Christology of the Fourth Gospel through a study of the titles which have been given to Jesus. We are aware that this is a limited way to approach the question, but it must be true that the names given to Jesus indicate his significance for John. It would be dangerous, however, to limit ourselves to Christological titles, as it is so easy for us to read our own ideas into them. The titles for Jesus in the New Testament became the categories which later Councils of the Church used, but each age alters the sense of these titles in the light of its own experience of Christ and his Church. To keep ourselves within the contours of John's world we open our argument with a study of the origin and the unique nature of the Fourth Gospel. Only then can we attempt to discover Jesus as the Logos, the Son of God, the Son of Man and the Christ, passing from pre-existence to his final glory with the Father through his incarnation and his 'hour'.

I wish to express my thanks to Frs Wally Cornell, S.D.B., and Kevin O'Leary, S.D.B., who read the whole of the manuscript in a first draft. In a special way, I am grateful to my brothers, John and Ray, who also read the manuscript at various stages. As 'ordinary folk', unaccustomed to the jargon of the professional scholar, their suggestions have been particularly helpful. My sister, Pauline, typed the whole of the manuscript twice: once from my impossible written notes, and then from a much corrected typescript. This little book has thus been a 'family effort', and I gratefully dedicate it to John, Ray and Pauline.

Salesian Theological College
Oakleigh 3166, Australia   Francis J. Moloney, S.D.B.
January 31st, 1977

---

1. C. H. Dodd, *The Present Task in New Testament Studies* (Cambridge, University Press, 1936).

2. See B. Lindars, *Behind the Fourth Gospel, Studies in Creative Criticism* 3 (London, SPCK, 1971), p. 11: 'The literature on it is immense, and even a scholar who devotes all his time to the study of the New Testament cannot hope to keep up with it.'

3. Some are available. The early chapters of W. F. Howard, *Christianity According to St. John* (London, Duckworth, 1943) are still valuable, as are sections of E. M. Sidebottom, *The Christ of the Fourth Gospel* (London, SPCK, 1961) and J. E. Davey, *The Jesus of St. John* (London, Lutterworth, 1958). Throughout this work we use 'John' and 'St John' to speak of the author and the book. We do not wish to indicate thereby any conviction about the precise nature of the author(s).

Chapter 1

THE ORIGIN AND THE UNIQUE NATURE
OF THE JOHANNINE GOSPEL

One of the most important contributions which modern biblical research has made to the interpretation of the New Testament, and especially of the Gospels, is an emphasis on theological, rather than historical, questions. There is always a problem involved, as the historical origin of the Christian message can easily be lost in the interpreter's search for an 'existential' understanding of the text, but modern research is surely correct when it insists that the Gospels are primarily theological documents. If one reads the Gospels carefully, one finds that it is impossible to trace a simple historical picture of the life of Jesus, to summarise what he said, or to indicate his movements with any certainty.

Matt 5.1-7,28, for example, contains what is commonly called the 'Sermon on the Mount'. Matthew sets the scene for the discourse by telling his readers: 'Seeing the crowds, he *went up on the mountain*, and when he sat down *his disciples* came to him. And he opened his mouth and taught *them*, saying . . .' (Matt 5.1-2). The sermon then proceeds, uninterrupted, until 7.28, where Matthew concludes: 'And when Jesus finished these sayings, *the crowds* were astonished at his teaching.' Was he speaking to his disciples, after leaving the crowds (as in 5.1-2), or were the crowds present all the time (as in 7.28)? In the Gospel of Matthew there are three chapters devoted to the sermon, which contains almost all the moral injunctions of Jesus. His disciples and/or the crowds are told clearly what is demanded of them if they are to follow Christ. This significant discourse, given solemnly on the top of a mountain, must have marked a memorable day in the public life of Jesus. However, if we look in the Gospels of Mark and John we will find no trace of such a day. In Lk 6.17-49 we do find it, but Luke sets the scene in the following way: 'And he *came down* with them and stood on a *level place*, with a *great*

9

multitude of people from all Judea and Jerusalem and the seacoast of Tyre and Sidon, who came to hear him and to be healed of their diseases; and those who were troubled with unclean spirits were cured. And all the crowd sought to touch him, for power came forth from him and healed them all.' The discourse then follows for 32 verses, in a version which abbreviates what Matthew's Gospel has reported quite considerably.

Was it on a mountain — or on a level place? Was it to his disciples — to an unspecified crowd — or to a great multitude of people, including non-Jews (Tyre and Sidon), who sought to hear his word and be cured? Did he say all that we find in the three chapters of Matthew — or only the 32 verses of Luke? Why is there no trace of the discourse in Mark and John? If we are determined to understand the Gospels as a 'Life of Jesus', as we of the twentieth century understand the 'life' of any great person, these are unsurmountable difficulties. The solution to the problem, however, is found in what was probably the very first line of the very first Gospel: Mark 1.1. This first verse runs: 'The beginning of the *Gospel* of Jesus Christ, the Son of God.' We are not told that the book which this verse prefaces is going to be a life story, but a 'gospel'. The Greek work for 'gospel' is *evangelion*, which does not mean 'life story', but 'good news'.[1] The Evangelists had no intention of writing a twentieth-century 'Life of Jesus'; they had something quite different to do: to proclaim Jesus as the Christ, the Son of God, and to tell us the good news of salvation which he had wrought by his death and resurrection. How they did this was largely conditioned by the particular needs of the ecclesial community in which the Evangelist lived, and for whom he wrote, but here we must also remember another important fact, too often neglected by modern scholars. In compiling their various versions of the 'good news' about Jesus, who was the Christ, the Son of God, the Evangelists went back to words and events from the life of Jesus

---

1. In fact, 'Gospel' comes from the Old English 'god-spel', meaning 'good news'.

himself. Jesus' words and deeds had been passed on by word of mouth (called 'oral tradition'); they were recalled in the community's liturgical celebrations, and some of them may have been written down in documents which we no longer possess.[2] This is the place where the Evangelists found the 'traditions' which stand behind their written Gospels. Each one of them used these traditions in his own particular way, but they took them from the memory of the life and teaching of Jesus. The Gospels *do* tell us about the historical Jesus, but they were never intended to be *the* life of Jesus.[3]

Once we are prepared to accept that the Gospels are primarily theological documents, using words and events from the life of Jesus for their own particular purpose, then the problem of the sermon on the mount or the plain vanishes. Matthew is very concerned with Israel and the Old Testament people of God. He is anxious to show that Jesus has not broken with the chosen people, but has established the 'True Israel', the continuation of the people of God in a new foundation, the fulfilment and the perfection of the promises made to Israel. Jesus, therefore, often appears as the new and perfect Moses. The most important event in the history of Israel was the Covenant, given on Mt Sinai; so now in Matt 5.1-7,28, the new Moses, Jesus, lays down the new law for the new people of God, which is but the *perfection* of the old Law (see especially Matt 5.17-48), and to do this he goes up on a mountain and from that new Sinai proclaims the new Law to the new people of God. The mountain is not just a historical note, but a profoundly important theological comment.

Luke's problem was different. As time passed, the newly-born Christian Church had to face the reality that their task

---

2. The sermon on the mount/plain, found only in Matthew and Luke, may show this. Scholars call the material common to Matthew and Luke, but not found in Mark (or John), 'Q', from the German word 'Quelle', meaning 'source'.

3. A fuller explanation of this is given by J. Ashton, *Why Were the Gospels Written?*, Theology Today 15 (Cork, Mercier Press, 1973).

still lay ahead of them. Jesus was not going to return in the very near future to destroy their opponents, to win over all opposition, and to reward the faithful, as Mark, especially, seemed to believe (see Mk 9.1 and ch. 13). Luke had to convince his readers that in their task, which was to go on into the unpredictable future, the spirit of Jesus was with them, guiding them through that future, in which the good news of Jesus would have to be brought to all men. Thus Luke places Jesus on a plain, available to all who would come to him, preaching to people from non-Jewish nations. He preached his new moral code to all who wished to hear his word, and he brought a message of healing, of forgiveness, love and kindness.

Which is the correct setting for the giving of the new Law of Christ? If we claim that the Gospels are historical in the modern sense of the term, then either Luke or Matthew is wrong. But this is not the case. They are both correct, as they are two equally valid presentations of the mystery of Christ, which the Church will continue to plumb until the end of time. We must not try to harmonise them, as we would thus lose a great deal of the authentic revelation of God, given to us authoritatively in the various books of the New Testament. The point should be clear from this simple example. Unless we are prepared to understand the Gospels as theological documents, we both impoverish our understanding of God's revelation to us through the New Testament, and we do an injustice to the theological significance of each single Gospel.

If this is the case with Matthew, Mark and Luke, what can be said of the Gospel according to John, which Clement of Alexandria once described as 'the spiritual Gospel'?[4] Even at a first cursory reading it is clear that John is very different from the other three Gospels. It is easy to place Matthew, Mark and Luke side by side and compare them with one another, but John hardly ever fits into their schemes.[5] What is the relation-

4. Reported by Eusebius, *Ecclesiastical History*, VI. 14. 7.

5. This is what is meant by 'Synoptic'. The three earlier Gospels can be placed side by side and compared with one glance.

ship between John and the other Gospels of the early Church? The Fourth Gospel moves around three visits to Jerusalem (chs 5; 7.10-10.42; 13-20). The Synoptic Gospels, on the other hand, have Jesus beginning his public ministry in Galilee, carrying out most of his work there, and only moving towards Jerusalem for a final passover feast, where he meets his death (see Mk 11-16.9; Matt 21-28.15; Lk 19.21-24.53). Many scholars conclude from this that John is not only an Evangelist with a well-developed theology but that he also may, at times, be closer to the history of Jesus of Nazareth, as it appears more than likely that Jesus did visit Jerusalem more regularly than he is allowed in the Synoptic traditions. Perhaps there are events in the Fourth Gospel which are closer to historical fact than is sometimes allowed.

John is not concerned with a multiplicity of miracles. Hardly a chapter goes by in the Synoptic narratives without some miracle being performed, and the Evangelists often concluded a section with a general statement about many people coming to Jesus with their ailments and being immediately cured, as if this was a regular event in the day to day life of Jesus (see, for example, Mk 6.55-56; Matt 5.24; Lk 6.17-19). John's miracles, however, though few in number, are more spectacular and dramatically reported. One man has been dead for four days (ch. 11), another paralysed for 38 years (ch. 5), and another blind from birth (ch. 9). Jesus made about 120 gallons of wine (ch. 2), and in the story of the walking on the water (ch. 6) an extra miracle is told which is not mentioned in the Synoptic Gospels: the boat was still in the middle of the stormy sea, but when they took Jesus aboard, all problems were solved 'and immediately the boat reached the land they were making for' (6.21). There are fewer miracles, but they are more impressive; they lead to discussion and generally serve as a springboard for a lengthy Johannine discourse (see especially chs. 5 and 6).

John has no story of the temptation of Jesus, no transfiguration; there is no scene in the garden of Gethsemani, no confession of Peter at Caesarea Philippi, and no institution of the Eucharist, despite the lengthy section given to the Last

Supper and its ensuing discourses (chs. 13-17). Yet there are hints of nearly all these Synoptic stories (see ch. 12 for the temptation and Gethsemani, 6.51-58 for the institution of the Eucharist, and 6.66-71 for Peter's confession). There is a marked difference in the structure and the material of the Fourth Gospel, yet one feels that there is some link with the older traditions.

It had been generally held that John knew the Synoptic Gospels, but this has been questioned since the work of P. Gardner-Smith.[6] He asked 'whether it is easier to account for the similarities between St John and the Synoptics without a theory of literary dependence, or to explain the discrepancies if such a theory has been accepted.'[7] He concluded that literary independence was the most satisfactory solution. The debate continues, but there is a growing consensus of opinion that John drew on a tradition which had grown independently. There are links because all the traditions go back to a pre-literary stage where there may have been considerable contact, but we can only speculate about the nature of these very early traditions. The discussion is still unresolved, but the idea of an independent Johannine tradition appears to be the most satisfactory working hypothesis. Not only does it resolve more of the problems produced by the combination of close literary parallels and the lack of them, but if John had known the Synoptic Gospels, why do we have in the Fourth Gospel such a different literary production? Would he not have been conscious that he was breaking sharply with the Gospels which had gone before him? There seems to be little evidence of this. It is not satisfactory to speak of John's 'completing' the traditional Gospels, as did some of the Fathers (Clement of Alexandria, Eusebius and Augustine).[8] Equally unconvincing is the suggestion of H. Windisch that John wished to replace the other Gospels by writing a final form of the Gospel.[9] We must allow the Fourth Gospel to stand alone, as it appears to

6. P. Gardner-Smith, *St. John and the Synoptic Gospels* (Cambridge, University Press, 1938).

7. *ibid.*, p.x.

be the product of its own particular traditions.

At this point we must ask: did John, the son of Zebedee, write this Gospel? If we admit that ch. 21 is not a part of the original Gospel (a fact now universally admitted), 'there is not a word in the whole Gospel to suggest that it is, or claims to be, by the Apostle John.'[10] In fact, the contrary is the case. If we did not have Jn 21.24-25, we would hardly expect the author to keep referring to himself as 'the beloved disciple'. A close study of the passages which deal with this unnamed disciple reveals that there are three different types of reference to a disciple who is never given a name. This can be seen from the following scheme:

1. In 1.37-42 there are two disciples of John who follow Jesus. One of them is named as Andrew — the other remains unnamed.

2. In other parts of the Gospel, there is a further reference to a man called continually 'the other disciple' (*ho allos mathetes:* 18.15,16; 20.3,4,8).

3. Yet another term for this enigmatic figure is the disciple 'whom Jesus loved" (*hon egapa ho Iesous*: 13.23; 19.26; 20.2). In 20.2 it looks as if the words 'whom Jesus loved' have been added to the reference to the man known as 'the other disciple'. This is a hint that these various names for one of the disciples were the result of the reflection of the Johannine church.

---

8. As reported by Eusebius, *Ecclesiastical History*, VI. 14. 7. Clement of Alexandria maintained that, 'Last of all, aware that the physical facts had been recorded in the gospels, encouraged by his pupils and irresistibly moved by the Spirit, John wrote a spiritual gospel.' See also, Eusebius, *op.cit.*, III. 24; Augustine, *De consensu evangelistarum*, IV. 10. 11ff.

9. H. Windisch, *Johannes und die Synoptiker. Wollte der vierte Evangelist die älteren Evangelien ergänzen oder ersetzen?* (Leipzig, Hinrichs, 1926).

10. B. H. Streeter, *The Four Gospels, A Study of Origins* (London, Macmillan, 1924), p. 431.

The clearest indication to us that this reference to the ideal disciple whom Jesus loved is a later development comes from ch. 21, which is universally admitted as redactional. Here the term 'whom Jesus loved' is used in every reference to the unknown disciple (see 21.7,20). From this evidence we can trace three clearly distinct stages in the development of the references to an eye-witness who, according to the redactional note in 21.24-25, stands behind the whole of the Fourth Gospel.

1st Stage: A disciple's reticence to speak about himself. This is probably historical, and this is the stage referred to by Jn 21.24-25, as well as the later tradition of the Church.

2nd Stage: As the tradition grows, a formula, recalling the reticence of the disciple and faithful to it, is fixed in the Johannine tradition: *ho allos mathetes*: 'the other disciple'.

3rd Stage: The elevation, on the part of the disciple's followers, interpreters and final editors, who held him in great esteem. Although remaining incognito, he is now presented as the model disciple, and thus can be called the one whom Jesus loved. He is not just a symbol, but a historical figure, idealised by his admiring followers, who look to him as their father in the faith and their model of true discipleship. As such they can justifiably call him the one 'whom Jesus loved'.

The *writer* intended to distinguish himself from the Beloved Disciple who, in an earlier, more modest tradition, was referred to as "the other disciple" (see 18.15-16; 20.2-10), and we would have inferred that he stood in much the same relation to the Beloved Disciple as Mark stood to Peter. From the evidence of the Gospel itself, we maintain that the Gospel was not *written* by the Beloved Disciple, who has now become not only an outstanding historical figure, but also an idealised model of the perfect disciple. It is the experience and understanding of this figure which is relayed to us through the Gospel. The Gospel, however, was *written* by someone to whom that disciple of Jesus was an object of reverent admiration. In the light of the many literary difficulties of this piece of writing, however, we have to go further than just one single *writer*. It is probably more correct to say that the Fourth Gospel is the product of several various editorial stages, finally unified into the Gospel as we have it now in the context of a 'Johannine School'. We can, therefore, speak of a disciple of Jesus as the *author*, in the sense that he is the *authority* behind the Gospel, even if he cannot be identified with the *writer*. It is important that this distinction between *author* and *writer*, so common to the men of the first century, but so strange to us, be properly understood, as this is probably the explanation of the traditional teaching about apostolic *authorship*.

The external evidence about the authorship is difficult to assess, as it is contradictory. Perhaps the most significant fact is that St. Ignatius of Antioch, who died about 110 A.D., and who wrote seven letters on his way to martyrdom, addressed two of his letters to the *Apostolic* Sees of Ephesus and Rome. The letter to Rome contains a possible allusion to the connection of that Church with Peter and Paul (*Romans*, 3.1), while the letter to the Ephesians goes out of the way to emphasise their special claim to be an Apostolic foundation on account of the particular affection shown to them by Paul (*Ephesians*, 12,2). If Ignatius had ever heard of a long residence and death of the Apostle John at Ephesus, it is very remarkable, given that Ephesus appears to be the most likely place of origin for the Gospel, that he should make no reference to it in that particular context.

On the other hand, Irenaeus, writing against the heretics about 180-200 A.D., says that, after the writing of the others Gospels, John, the disciple of the Lord who reclined on his bosom (see Jn 13.23; 21.20), published his Gospel at Ephesus (*Adv. Haer.*, III.1.1). About the same period various other witnesses to authorship by John, the disciple of the Lord, arise. By the end of the second century, there is a belief in the Johannine authorship of the Gospel. The question that remains unanswered is: were they correct? Perhaps Irenaeus was simply guessing that the unnamed disciple was John the Apostle. If Eusebius (*Ecclesiastical History*, IV.14.3-8) is correct, it would not be a guess, as Irenaeus received his information from Polycarp, Bishop of Smyrna, who had heard it from John himself, but the correctness of this chain of tradition has recently been seriously questioned. There is some evidence from tradition that John the Apostle died a martyr well before the end of the first century, but this may be the result of a confusion between John, son of Zebedee, and John the Baptist. The main difficulties which arise in any discussion of the external evidence stem from the fact that the Gnostic heretics found great support for their positions in the Fourth Gospel, and thus its place in the literature of the orthodox Church was threatened. Perhaps the linking of the Gospel to an apostolic author at the close of the second century was one of the means used to show that this Gospel was truly a part of the apostolic witness to Jesus, and not just a Gnostic source-book. This is probably the main reason for the insistence on Johannine authorship from Irenaeus onwards; but must we conclude from this that the tradition is wrong, or that there is no reason or logic in choosing John, the son of Zebedee, as the author of the spiritual Gospel? This is the tendency of modern scholarship, but it may be somewhat presumptuous.

Ultimately, our information is inconclusive — we cannot state anything as certainly proved. As a hypothesis, we would suggest that the Gospel is closely linked with a disciple of Jesus (John?) and he can be called the *author*. The written Gospel, as we have it today, however, is the product of what we have called a Johannine School, and I-III John and perhaps Revelation are evidence for the existence of this 'school'. But where, when and why was the Gospel written?

We have argued throughout that John is unique and must be considered as standing alone, despite certain literary affinities with the Synoptic tradition. It is so different that scholars in the past have attempted to put the writing of the Gospel well outside the Apostolic era. They argued that the well-developed understanding of Jesus as the Son of God in an almost metaphysical sense is fully Greek, and that the fully developed sacramental theology (see, for example, the eucharistic teaching of 6.51-58) showed a Church already well into

18

the second century. The use of certain terms: ascending and descending, light and darkness, life and death, living water, the bread of life, salvation, logos, etc., are also taken as an indication that John came into existence in the second century, as these terms are regarded as having come into Johannine language through Gnosticism, which only reached its full development in the second century.

This tendency to date the Fourth Gospel well into the second century has been exploded by some very important archaeological discoveries. In 1935 a fragment of papyrus, called the John Rylands papyrus, was published by C. H. Roberts. The papyrus, which came from central Egypt, must be dated about 130-140 A.D. On one side of the papyrus is Jn 18.31-33 and on the other side is Jn 18.37-38. It is clear from this that by 130 A.D. (and presumably earlier) the Fourth Gospel was being circulated in Egypt. The second important discovery was the Dead Sea Scrolls, from Qumran. Much of John's strange contrasting language: light and darkness, life and death etc., is found in the literature of the Jewish sect which was responsible for the documents found in the caves near the Essene monastery of Wadi Qumran, which came to a sudden end with the Romans conquest of 70 A.D. It remains true that many Johannine terms are found in Gnostic or semi-Gnostic documents, particularly in Mandaean literature and in the Hermetic literature, but the influence may have been from John to Gnosticism, and not vice-versa. Our first evidence of a Gnostic system comes from the second century. Perhaps it was nascent in the syncretistic world of Asia Minor. This may have led John to use some of the terms, but John cannot be called Gnostic.

There has been considerable interest shown in the possibility that the Fourth Gospel was originally in Aramaic, and thus linked even more closely with the earliest Church, which probably spoke Aramaic. The discussion has been long and complicated, and need not delay us here. Although it is too much to claim that John was originally written in Aramaic, there certainly seems to be a close link with many Jewish modes of thought and expression and a good knowledge of

Jewish feasts and topography. John's interests, however, range wider than those of Judaism. C. K. Barrett has summarised the situation satisfactorily when he writes: 'A Jewish element in the Fourth Gospel cannot be denied. The language recalls the Old Testament; the narratives, far from being allegorical inventions, are tied to topographical details. This Jewish element is, however, too weak to permit the conclusion that John wrote only for a Jewish audience or that his main intention was to transmit with precision a Palestinian tradition.'[11]

One of the most consistent features of the Gospel is a conflict with 'the Jews'. This is the clearest indication of why the Gospel was written. At the end of the first century, faced with a sect which confessed that Jesus of Nazareth was the Christ, the Synagogue at Javneh, by then the religious centre of Judaism, under the leadership of Gamaliel, called upon all faithful Jews to condemn the followers of Jesus of Nazareth in the context of a prayer called the 'eighteen benedictions'. The Benedictions were a part of the prayer of the Jewish synagogue service. The Rabbis at Javneh introduced the following 'Benediction': 'For apostates may there be no hope, and may the Nazarenes and the heretics suddenly perish.' Everyone had to pray this Benediction loudly. Thus, anyone who failed to do so was seen as believing that Jesus was the Christ and was to be turned out of the synagogue. This was a severe blow to Christians, since they saw their faith in Jesus as the Christ to be something which they could hold while they continued in their traditional Jewish practices.

In John 9 we see this drama of the Jewish-Christian Church in practice, in the story of the man born blind. The man's parents refused to answer the Jews' questions: 'because they feared the Jews, for the Jews had already agreed that if anyone should confess him to be the Christ, he was to be put out of the synagogue' (9.22). The term used to speak of the exclusion

---

11. C. K. Barrett, *The Gospel of John and Judaism* (London, SPCK, 1975), pp. 74-75. See his whole treatment of the question on pp. 20-75.

from synagogue worship is *aposunagogos*, used only by John (see also 12.42 and 16.2). In fact the man born blind confesses to the Jews (v.33): 'If this man were not from God, he could do nothing.' They reply by casting him out of the synagogue (v.34). 'John speaks of discipleship in terms of the conditions with which his readers were familiar.'[12] This is but one, admittedly the clearest, reference to the struggle that seems to have been in progress between the Johannine Church and the synagogue.

John Robinson has recently attempted to show that this is not the case, but that the Gospel had its origin among Greek-speaking Jews in Jerusalem and was finally published in Asia Minor to convert Greek-speaking Jews of the Diaspora, some time about 65 A.D.[13] His argument is not convincing. It does not do justice to the case we have argued. He merely claims that the Fourth Gospel reflects the rift between Church and Synagogue which was already taking place in the 40's and 50's. There may well have been a breach at this early stage but, as the texts which Robinson himself uses illustrate, it was caused by the Gentile mission. John's Gospel reflects a different situation, where a Christological problem has caused an irrevocable separation between Church and Synagogue. This is shown by the fact that only John uses the term *aposunagogos*. Robinson does not explain why this term *never* appears in the rest of the New Testament. It does not appear because John's

---

12. B. Lindars, *The Gospel of John*, New Century Bible (London, Oliphants, 1972), p. 347. For the history of the 'Eighteen Benedictions' and the conflict which the insertion of the 'Benediction against the heretics' caused, see G. F. Moore, *Judaism in the First Centuries of the Christian Era* (Cambridge, Harvard University Press, 1958), I, pp. 289-296; J. L. Martyn, *History and Theology in the Fourth Gospel* (New York, Harper and Row, 1968), pp. 17-40, and especially S. Pancaro, *The Law in the Fourth Gospel. The Torah and the Gospel Moses and Jesus, Judaism and Christianity according to John*, Supplements to Novum Testamentum XLII (Leiden, E. J. Brill, 1975), pp. 247-253; 494-497; 510-514.

13. J. A. T. Robinson, *Redating the New Testament* (London, SCM Press, 1976), pp. 254-311.

situation was different. His community was experiencing a total expulsion from Judaism, not some lesser exclusion from synagogue worship.[14] It is to a community struggling for survival in a hostile Jewish world that at least part of the Johannine message is directed. One must be careful, however, not to limit the Gospel to this conflict. There is a great deal of contact with nascent Gnosticism, and a universal outlook which takes the reader beyond the Jewish-Christian problem, especially in the discourses from 13.31 to 17.26. Even this, however, may be linked with the separation of the Christians from the synagogue, as they were now *forced* to understand their role in a more universal context. We must place the composition of the Fourth Gospel in a cosmopolitan world, where the Johannine community had the dual task of resolving the problem with Judaism, and adapting themselves to the multi-cultural influences in which they lived.

We are faced now with some established facts and other reasonable working hypotheses:

(a) The external evidence of John Rylands papyrus and the language of Qumran.

(b) A link with the earliest Gospel tradition.

(c) A link with the Jewish world, yet an important opening to the problems and language of the Mediterranean world at large.

(d) The evidence that the Gospel has gone through several stages of editorial activity, but was originally linked with 'a disciple' of Jesus.

(e) A strong tradition, starting late in the second century, linking the Gospel with John, the son of Zebedee, and with the city of Ephesus.

---

14. See W. Schrage, Article *'aposunagogos'*, *TDNT* VII (1971) pp. 848-852. This thorough article (not mentioned in Robinson's book) concludes: 'To think in terms of a lesser ban is a trivialising; this is no mere excommunication but total expulsion, a result of the birkath ha-minim' (p. 852). The 'birkath ha-minim' is the Hebrew for 'Benediction against the Heretics' of Javneh.

In the light of the above, we feel that, while fully aware that we cannot be certain, a Johannine School eventually wrote the Fourth Gospel at Ephesus (see Justin, *Dialogue with Trypho*, 81.4; Eusebius, *Ecclesiastical History*, III.23.1-4; IV.18.6-8; V.24.3), where there is proof of a strong Jewish presence in the midst of a highly cosmopolitan world which naturally gathered in this flourishing seaport (see Rev 2.9; 3.9 and Acts 19.1-7). The Gospel must have reached its final form about 100 A.D.

The Fourth Gospel has been described as a pool in which a child can play and an ocean in which an elephant can swim. It is at once complicated in detail, yet simple in its structure and purpose, as can be seen from our proposed structure of the Gospel:

I *Prologue:* 'Designed to enable the reader to understand the doctrines of the book' (R. H. Lightfoot).[15]

1.1-18

II *The Book of Signs:* The public manifestation of the revelation of God in the human activity of Jesus.   *1.19-12.50*

  i. The opening days of the revelation of Jesus and the hopes that they bring. NB: The final promise from Jesus, that what follows will be the revelation of even 'greater things' than those hoped for (1.50-51).

1.19-51

  ii. From Cana to Cana: The question of the correct type of faith, as is indicated by John's redactional note in 2.23-25. The action evolves in the following fashion:

Jesus' Mother (correct faith)
- (a) The Jews (no faith)
- (b) Nicodemus (incomplete faith)
- (c) John the Baptist (correct faith)
- (a1) Samaritan Woman (no faith)

---

15. R. H. Lightfoot, *St. John's Gospel* (London, Oxford University Press, 1956), p. 11.

This unique piece of literature was written at the end of the Apostolic era for many reasons. The memory of the living Jesus was passing away and the Gospel of Jesus Christ, now preached throughout the Mediterranean world, was coming face to face with the powerful intellectual currents of the time, especially Gnosticism, and the scandal of a God who became man. This concept was foreign to Greek culture, which had its own ideas about incarnate deities. Generally one of the hierarchy of gods from Olympus merely pretended to take human form — very often for some sort of sexual motive — but they could never be regarded as truly incarnate. This God of the Christians must have merely taken the form of a man, they argued, as a God could never be lifted up on a Cross. Against this, John insists that the Word became flesh (1.14; I John 1.1-4), without ceasing to be truly God (see, for example, 10.30: 'I and the Father are one'). This balancing of the human and the divine in the Fourth Gospel is one of the features which makes it unique among the Gospels. However, we must be careful lest we make the Gospel the mere product of its surroundings. Like the other Gospels, it is closely linked with a pre-literary tradition, but more important than all this, the Gospel according to John is the product of a mind which had an extraordinarily penetrating insight into who Jesus was, and what he had done for the salvation of mankind.

The Fourth Gospel is a book with a message. The author wants to bring his reader to the point of decision. As he says in 20.30-31, he had written his work 'that you may believe that Jesus is the Christ, the Son of God, and that believing you may have life in his name.' This purpose is expressed with equal clarity in the miniature gospel of 3.16: 'For God so loved the world that he gave his only Son, that whoever believes in him should not perish but have eternal life.' These are not vague statements. Two possibilities are presented: 'to perish' or 'to have eternal life'. John knows no middle course. He sees mankind as inexorably faced with these solemn alternatives. Man is involved in a power-struggle between cosmic forces. On one side is the darkness (more often called 'blindness', 'evil', 'this world' or 'the prince of this world'); to commit oneself to these powers leads to destruction and death. On the other side is the light (associated with 'sight', 'the Spirit', 'the water of life', 'the bread of life' and 'the light of the world'). All of this is revealed in Jesus Christ, and commitment to him, in faith, leads to 'salvation' and 'life'. Consequently, the decision a man makes either for light or darkness affects his whole existence. The freedom of man is very important for John. He never presents Jesus as a judge, coming to condemn man, but as 'the truth' which stands before man as 'the light'. Man himself must make the choice. No pressure is brought to bear in John's Gospel — man is free, and judges himself by his own decision for or against the revelation of God in and through Jesus Christ.

John believes passionately in making one's own decision about Jesus Christ. This is because the appearance of Jesus on the historical plane is the irruption of the light from the divine realm into the created order where darkness and evil are rampant. The power-struggle is fought out, not only at a cosmic level, as it was in the Gnostic myths, but also in the historic events of the life of Jesus. This is why John decided to write a 'Gospel' . . . a form of literature which conveyed its message about Jesus Christ through a life-story. In this strife the Cross is central. It is the hour: 'The hour has come for the Son of Man to be glorified' (12.23), and 'Now is the Son of Man glorified and in him God is glorified' (13.31). It is 'the hour' when the powers of darkness appear to have brought their enemy down, but with magnificent irony John shows that it is precisely in 'the hour' that the Son of Man is victoriously glorified, revealing the Father for all men to gaze upon, and thus to be saved (see 19.37).[16]

---

16. See B. Lindars, *John*, pp. 24-25.

Chapter 2

THE LOGOS

1. *The origin of Jn 1.1-18 and its role in the Gospel as a whole*

We have already insisted that one of the major contributions of modern critical exegesis has been the recognition of the various theological positions of the Evangelists. One of the most popular ways of identifying this position is to attempt to locate the 'source' of the Evangelist's material, and thus to see how he has refashioned it for his own theological purposes. In fact, this is what we did in our short reference to the sermon on the mount/plain. The material of the discourse was probably found by both Matthew and Luke in their common source 'Q'. Both Matthew and Luke, however, by their own editorial comments (see Matt 5.1-2; Lk 6.17-19) and their different uses of the same material from 'Q', had a different point to make in their use of that material. The sermon on the mount/plain is one of the easier examples. Turning now to consider the origin ('source') of the Johannine Prologue (1.1-18), we are looking into one of the most difficult and discussed questions in New Testament scholarship.

Although these verses form the opening section of a Christian Gospel, there are scholars who claim that they had their origin outside Christianity. The most outstanding proponent of this theory is Rudolf Bultmann.[1] He is convinced that the Prologue stands apart from the Gospel. It cannot be regarded as an introduction, but is rather like an 'overture'. Behind the hymn stand two elements:

i. A wisdom myth. This so-called myth links the creator-Wisdom with the world, as she comes to earth to live among men but is refused, and thus returns to her place of origin.

---

1. R. Bultmann, *The Gospel of John. A Commentary* (Oxford, Basil Blackwell, 1971), pp. 13-83.

ii. The Gnostic redeemer myth. This myth spoke of a heavenly redeemer who revealed the knowledge (Greek: *gnosis*)
of the truth to men. This knowledge lights the spark of life
in man, thus saving him from the evil chaos of creation.

Bultmann claims that the Prologue was formed from these
two elements. It is a pre-Christian Gnostic hymn, having its
origin in a Mandaean sect which honoured John the Baptist, as
the surviving Mandaeans (they live in small groups in Iran and
Iraq) do today. This hymn was taken over by Christians who
played down the role of the Baptist (see vv. 6-8,15) and the
Logos was identified with Jesus (as can be seen from the
additions to v. 12b: 'who believed in his name', added to
christianise vv. 12c-13; and vv. 17-18, which introduce 'Jesus
Christ', not mentioned until this point). This opinion had
support in the 1920's and 30's from scholars who belonged to
the 'History of Religions School' in their attempt to understand the New Testament almost exclusively in the light of
ancient religions and culture.[2]

The presuppositions of the History of Religions School,
however, have been seriously questioned and today there is
hardly a scholar who would accept the theory of Bultmann in
its entirety. The hymn must always have been Christian, and if
so there could be two possible sources:

i. The hymn comes from a collection of Christian hymns,
one of which John has taken and adapted for his own use.
It is commonly accepted that there are various passages in
the New Testament which were originally hymns in the
early Christian Church. The most famous example of this
is Phil 2.6-11, which most scholars see as an early Christian
hymn, perhaps originally in Aramaic, which Paul has taken
over and adapted for his own purposes. The same thing
may have happened with the Johannine Prologue. Scholars
point to the fact that the title 'Logos' never appears again
in the Gospel, and that there are certain stylistic traits; use
of words which only appear here, and possibly a strophic

---

2. See, especially, R. Bultmann, *Primitive Christianity in
its Contemporary Setting* (London, SCM Press, 1956).

structure, which indicate that John has taken the hymn from a source of hymns. However, there are too many essentially Christian themes (especially the incarnation) to claim that the hymn was originally Gnostic. It must be from a Christian source.

ii. The hymn is the composition of the Evangelist, possibly re-edited at a later stage by the Evangelist himself or by another. The themes of the Prologue: pre-existence (vv. 1-2), incarnation (vv. 5,9-14), the revelation of God in Jesus (vv. 14-18) and the gaining of life through faith in this revelation (vv. 12,16), are not foreign to the Gospel, but are essential to a proper understanding of its narrative. 'The Johannine Prologue . . . serves the same function as its Marcan equivalent; without it the chapters which follow are incomprehensible to us, as to the Jewish opponents in the story.'[3] This is a part of Johannine technique. John's readers have been told the full truth about Jesus in the Prologue. They have been given the key which can unlock the whole mystery of the events and discourses which follow; but the disciples and the Jews do not have this key. To them it will be unfolded in the signs and discourses which are to follow, and which will bring them either to belief in or rejection of Jesus as the revealer and the revelation of God.

We are not prepared to accept that the hymn comes from a non-Christian source, but the other two possibilities both have elements in their favour. The possibility that there was an early Christian Logos-hymn, however, always remains speculative, as we have no evidence for the existence of such a hymn outside the Fourth Gospel. Some point to 1 Tim 3,16 and Heb 1,2-5, but these examples are too short to be called hymnic. Some parallels can be found in the *Odes of Solomon*, and this may be an indication that such a hymn was possible, but the Odes and the Fourth Gospel probably grew up in the same

---

3. M. D. Hooker, 'The Johannine Prologue and the Messianic Secret', *New Testament Studies* 21 (1974-75), p. 51. The article runs from pp. 40-58.

milieu, without having any direct influence upon one another. While the Odes should not be regarded as one of John's sources, they do show how some of the literature of the period was being written.

A serious objection can be raised against the methods of the scholars who argue for a previous Christian hymn as a source. If the source which has to be recovered is a hymn, then various passages in the Prologue which break into the hymnic structure of the passage, especially vv. 6-8,15, which refer, in a quasi-narrative form, to John the Baptist, have to be eliminated. Similarly, anything clearly 'Johannine' must also be eliminated, so that we can discover the pre-Johannine source.

It is, however, a dangerous circular argument to eliminate all the Johannine elements and then claim to have discovered a non-Johannine source. What has happened is the *creation*, not the *recovery* of this source. The most obvious 'additions', those referring to John the Baptist, tie the whole of the Prologue to history. They may be clumsily inserted, but they serve a purpose which the interpreter must respect.

Nevertheless, it does appear that there may have been some form of 'source', which was linked with Wisdom speculation behind the Prologue. However, it is impossible to find the exact structure and meaning of that source. What we have in Jn 1.1-18 is intimately linked with the Gospel as a whole. It is the essential, if extraordinary, opening to this extraordinary example of the literary form of 'Gospel'. It is, as Lightfoot has claimed: 'the key to the understanding of the Gospel'.[4] Once we have grasped the message of the Prologue, we can make sense of Jesus' miracles, and especially his discourses. If we have not understood the Prologue, the Gospel will read like the story of some mysterious demi-God who has no real authority to ask that men believe in him.

---

4. R. H. Lightfoot, *St John*, p. 11. See also C. K. Barrett, *The Gospel according to St John* (London, S.P.C.K., 1955), p. 130: 'John intends that the whole of his Gospel shall be read in the light of this verse (v. 1). The deeds and words of Jesus are the deeds and words of God; if this be not true the book is blasphemous.'

2. *The origin of the term 'Logos'*

Only the Prologue of the Fourth Gospel speaks of Jesus as the 'Logos' (Word). The discussions around the origin of the term are highly complex, and we can only hope to survey briefly the various points of view, before coming to some conclusions of our own.

I - From the Greek or Hellenistic World

i. Heraclitus lived in Ephesus in the sixth century B.C., and was the first to use the term 'Logos' to speak of the fundamental and eternal principle which united all things and mankind. It was once claimed that this may have been an influence on John, but this is nowadays abandoned.

ii. In the time of the redaction of the Fourth Gospel Stoicism was one of the most popular philosophies. Although there appears to be little influence of Stoicism on Johannine thought (contrary to Pauline thought), some suggest that the Stoic idea of the 'Logos' played a part in John's choice of the term. According to the Stoics the 'Logos' was the soul of the world, the immanent divine principle. They distinguished between the 'internal word' = thought *(logos endiathetos)* and the 'external word' = speech *(logos prophorikos)*. Human reason was able to participate in the universal 'Logos' by means of the *logos endiathetos*.

iii. Philo Judaeus. Philo's works are an attempt to link the Old Testament faith of Israel with Hellenistic Philosophy (especially Stoicism). Between God and the world there are many intermediate *'logoi'*, among which there is a supreme *ho Logos*. It is not clear whether this Logos is a real and substantial being, or the personification of a divine attribute. It could be described as:

— The instrument of God in creation, the model of creation and the unifying principle of the world.
— The intermediary between God and the Universe, the means of God's revelation among men as the communication of the gifts of God. He is also the principle of a moral life.

— It is called: Word of God; first-born son of God; *'deuteros theos'*; legatus Dei.

Obviously we are closer to the Johannine use of the term here, but serious difficulties still remain:

(a) Philo's use of the term is fully Greek. For the Greek philosophers the Logos was first and foremost some sort of rational principle which governed and unified the universe. It is a metaphysical and cosmological principle. This is very different from the Johannine idea of the Word by which God speaks to men and reveals himself.

(b) The Philonic 'Logos' remains somewhat of an enigma. The personification and the pre-existence of the Logos is never very clear. These two elements — personification and pre-existence — are central to the Johannine concept.

iv. As we have already mentioned, for Bultmann the Logos hymn comes from a Gnostic background. Although occasional support is still found for this argument, the majority of scholars agree that the amazing collection of sources used (neopythagoreanism, neoplatonism, Ignatius of Antioch, Odes of Solomon, Mandaean literature, Jewish Wisdom speculation, Christian Gnostic sources etc.) do not prove the presence of a developed Gnostic myth of the redeemer in the first century.

II - From the Semitic World

Here there are several possibilities which may all, in fact, have played a part as background to the term 'Logos'.

i. 'The Word of the Lord'

The Hebrew *dabar* means not only 'word', but also 'thing', 'affair', 'event', 'action'. In Hebrew thought the concept of *dabar* had a certain *dynamic energy* (see Hos 1.1; Joel 1.1; Deut 32.46-47; Ps 107.20; Wisd 16.26) and *creative power* (see Ps 33.6; Wisd 9.1; Is 55.11; Ps 146.15,18).

ii. Personified Wisdom

Wisdom is never called the Word of God, but she comes from the mouth of God (see Ecclus 24.3; Wisd 9.1-2) from the beginning (Prov 8.22-23), is with God (Ecclus 1.1), an active agent in creation (Wisd 9.9; 7.22; Prov 8.27-30). It is also important to notice its connection with light and life in Prov 8.27-30 and Eccles 2.13. She came into the world to be rejected by men (Wisd 9.10; Prov 8.31; Ecclus 15.7; Bar 3.12) and she set up her tent among men (Ecclus 24.8-12). In the Old Testament presentation of Wisdom there are good parallels for almost every detail of the Prologue's description of the Word. The Prologue has carried personification further than did the Old Testament in describing Wisdom, but that development stems from the historical event of the incarnation. It is often asked why the hymn of the Prologue speaks of 'Word' rather than 'Wisdom', and the answer generally given is that in Greek the former is masculine, while the latter is feminine. The former was used of the person of Jesus Christ. There may be some truth in this, but it still has not answered the question why the term 'Logos' was chosen in preference to another term.

iii. Jewish speculation on the Law

Later Jewish speculation saw the Law (Torah) as having been created before all things and having served as the pattern on which God created the world (see Ecclus 24.22-32). The Torah is also presented as the Word of the Lord (see Is 2.3). There are various other parallels in Jewish literature where the Torah is presented as the Light and Life and as the supreme example of God's love.[5] Jn 1.17 may show that the Johannine doctrine of the Word was, at least in part, a Christian reaction and answer to the Jewish speculations on the Law. If our suggestions about the world which produced the Fourth Gospel are correct, then this possibility fits in well with the needs of the Johannine Community.

iv. The Targumic use of *Memra*

The Aramaic Bible, called the Targum, used *memra*

5. See C. H. Dodd, *The Interpretation of the Fourth Gospel* (Cambridge, University Press, 1954), pp. 82-83.

('word') to translate 'Word of the Lord', and as a surrogate for God himself. If the Aramaic expression for 'word' was used in the Targums as a paraphrase for God in his dealings with men, the author of the Prologue may have seen fit to use this title for Jesus who pre-eminently incorporates God's presence among men.

The Prologue's description of Jesus as the Word is far closer to biblical and Jewish strains of thought than it is to anything purely Hellenistic. In the mind of the theologian of the Prologue, it could well be that the Word of the Lord that came to the prophets had become personal in Jesus Christ, the embodiment of divine revelation. Jesus was also understood as divine Wisdom, pre-existent, but now come to teach and to give life. He is the *memra*, God's presence among men.

There is another important element in John's choice of the title which is often neglected. It could be that the title 'Logos' was the final development of the New Testament theme of the communication of God in the person of Jesus Christ. The title could come from John's important use of *legein* (to say) and *lalein* (to speak) in the discourses of Jesus and elsewhere. The Prologue, written after the Gospel, takes up this theme of the communication of God in and through the person of Jesus Christ by calling Jesus the Logos.

The Jewish and Christian background seems much closer to John's use of the term, but we must not completely ignore the Hellenistic world. We would suggest that John's theology of the Word receives its content from his own theological vision of Jesus as the authentic communication of the revelation of God, which has as its background Jewish and New Testament traditions, especially the Jewish Word-theology and Wisdom-speculation. However, remembering that John's audience was not *only* Jewish, the actual choice of the title 'Logos' (and not 'Sophia', Wisdom) was influenced by two factors:

(a) His own theological use of *legein* and *lalein* throughout the Gospel to indicate the communication of God in and through the Word of Jesus Christ.

(b) The abundant use of the term in the diaspora, in an

attempt to link Jewish traditions with Hellenistic culture. This is evidenced in the work of Philo. John probably did not know of Philo or his work, but there are similarities in both language and thought between Philo and the Fourth Gospel. The Fourth Gospel grew in the context of diaspora Judaism, and the works of Philo must be understood as our only complete indication of the philosophy and theology of the diaspora Jews who were attempting to integrate their traditional faith with Hellenistic thought. There is no direct influence of Philo on John, but Philo's use of 'Logos' (over 1200 times) indicates that the term was a favourite one in the world in which the Fourth Gospel received its final expression.

3. *The structure of the Prologue*

Attempts to structure the Prologue generally follow one of two methods.

I — A succession of ideas
II — Developing according to literary criteria, either
  i. moving round a central idea with the statement and restatement of themes before and after the presentation of that idea. This type of literary pattern is called a 'chiasm';
  or ii. moving in a spiral fashion, through some sort of circular development.

A few examples of each system will suffice to show that each has its merits and defects.

I — Structure according to ideas.

i. B. F. Westcott (1882)
  (1) The Word in his absolute, eternal being (v. 1)
  (2) The Word in relation to creation (vv. 2-18)
    — the essential facts (vv. 2-5)
    — the historic manifestation of the Word generally (vv. 6-13)
    — the Incarnation as apprehended by personal experience (vv. 14-18)

ii. M.-J. Lagrange (1927) and C. K. Barrett (1955)
  (1) The Word and its relationship to God, the world and

men (vv. 1-5)
(2) John, witness of the light (vv. 6-8)
(3) The light comes; how it is received (vv. 9-13)
(4) The Incarnation brings grace and truth (vv. 14-18)

Many other examples could be given, but this system does not explain why John the Baptist appears twice, and it suffers from being tied to a sort of time-line. It indicates the three modes of being of the Word: pre-existence, the Word as the Light of all people and the Incarnation. The appearance of the Baptist in vv. 6-8 is difficult, and the refusal of the Word in vv. 10-11 also goes unexplained — how is this refusal possible, as the Incarnation of the Word does not take place till v. 14?

II — Structure according to literary criteria

i. M.-E. Boismard: the structure of the Prologue around a central idea (a chiasm)

The Prologue moves like a parabola:

The Word of God vv. 1-2   v. 18 The Son in the
                                       Father

Its role in creation v. 3   v. 17 Role of re-creation
A gift to men vv. 4-5   v. 16 A gift to men
The witness of the   v. 15 Witness of the
Baptist vv. 6-8   Baptist
The coming of the Word   v. 14 The Incarnation
into the world vv. 9-11

vv. 12-13
Through the Incarnate Word,
we become Sons of God.

This structure is simple, ingenious and there certainly seems to be the repetition of themes in vv. 1 and 18; 6-8 and 15. However, some of the other parallels are forced. There is little relation between vv. 4-5 and 16. The idea of 'gift' and 'men' is not common to both sides of the chiasm. V. 17 does not speak of re-creation, which is a Pauline rather than a Johannine idea (see 2 Cor 15.17; Gal 6.15), but of grace and truth. Finally, this chiasm makes the fact that we become children of God the point of the Prologue. While this is important, the hymn is not to sing of this filiation, but of the incarnate Word.

ii. A cyclic, spiralling structure

We must not impose too strict a structure, but there does seem to be a movement of the thought and expression of the passage. Ideas are mentioned, they fade and they are then taken up again with renewed vigour — somewhat like the movement of waves on the seashore which rise, fall and fade, only to be replaced by another wave which carries the thought further.

We have found the most satisfactory application of this principle in the work of S. A. Panimolle and I. de la Potterie.[6] They suggest that the Prologue is structured in three parallel developments. The first section opens with a consideration of the Word in God, but the two following sections, both of which are concerned with the Word in history, open with a reference to John the Baptist. In this way, the speculations of the Prologue are firmly anchored in history. The major divisions are:

I — vv. 1- 5: Introduction: The Word.

II — vv. 6-14: Central statement: The insertion of the Word into the history of salvation.

III — vv. 15-18: Conclusion: The revealing role of the Word — Jesus Christ — for all who believe.

Inside these major sections there are four themes which are developed:

(a) The Word, announced and described.

6. S. A. Panimolle, *Il Dono della Legge e la Grazia della Verita*, Teologia Oggi 21 (Rome, Editrice AVE, 1973), pp. 71-105; I. de la Potterie, *Exegesis Quarti Evangelii: Prologus S. Johannis* (Rome, Pontifical Biblical Institute: cyclostyled notes, 1974-75), pp. 13-23. Anyone who has followed Fr de la Potterie's classes will quickly recognise the influence which his thought has had on my presentation of the Johannine Prologue. I gratefully acknowledge this influence, and beg pardon for my own aberrations.

(b) The coming of the revelation of the Word into the world.
(c) The gift of the Word to men — and man's reply.
(d) The nature of the gift: a free gift which is truth.

Not all the major sections (I, II and III) contain all the themes (a, b, c and d), but they are all contained and fully developed in the central section of the Prologue, i.e., vv. 6-14.

The Prologue, then, is structured in the following fashion:

I — *Introduction*
(vv. 1-5)
The Word.

(a) The Word in God (vv. 1-2)
(b) The Word's revealing role as the light of men (vv. 3-4).
(c) The light of men and the impotency of the darkness (v. 5).

II — *Central Section*
(vv. 6-14)
The insertion of the Word into the history of salvation.

(a) The insertion of the Word into history through the historical witness of John the Baptist to the light (vv. 6-8).
(b) The light comes into the world (v. 9).
(c) The dual reply of men:
 - negative (vv. 10-11).
 - positive (vv. 12-13).
(d) The gift of the incarnate Son - a free gift which is truth (v. 14).

III — *Conclusion*
(vv. 15-18)
The revealing role of the Word, Jesus Christ, in the history of all of us who believe.

(a) The activity of the Baptist among men, witnessing to the pre-existent Word (v. 15).
(c) The gift of God to all of us (v. 16).

> (d) The concrete gift of Jesus
>   Christ in relation to the
>   gift of the Law - Jesus
>   Christ as a free gift which
>   is truth (vv. 17-18).

4. *The Prologue: John 1,1-18*

We must turn now to an examination of the whole of Jn
1.1-18. Only after we have done this can we hope to be able to
formulate some sort of explanation of the significance of the
Johannine description of Jesus as the Logos. Although this
title appears only in the Prologue, it is vital for a correct
understanding of the Johannine Jesus.

R. H. Lightfoot, a great English scholar, wrote: '1.1-18,
usually called the prologue, is designed to enable the reader to
understand the doctrines of the book.'[7] Here we are given the
key which can unlock the whole mystery of the chapters
which follow. There are three groups involved in the drama of
faith: Jesus, his interlocutors *and* the readers! We the readers,
know about this man, Jesus, and where he comes from, but
the Jews and the disciples — the actors in the historical drama
which unfolds throughout the story of the Gospel — are in the
dark! To them it will be unfolded in the signs and discourses
which are to·take place — culminating in the cry of faith from
Thomas — 'My Lord and my God' (20.28). But we, the
readers of John's version of the 'good news', are introduced to
it by means of a hymn to the Incarnate Son of God, Jesus
Christ, which is unparalleled in the rest of the New Testament.

I — INTRODUCTION: The Word (vv. 1-5)
(a) The Word in God (vv. 1-2)

> 'In the beginning was the Word and the Word was
> with God, and the Word was God. He was in the
> beginning with God.'

John shows right from the very first verse that what he is
really interested in telling us is the relationship which God
has set up between himself and man — this is why he

---

7. R. H. Lightfoot, *St John*, p. 11.

chooses to name the Son of God who will become flesh 'the Word'. The title of its very nature implies a revelation ... a divine communication. How valid will this revelation be? The most valid that one could possibly ask for, because the word 'was with (?) God' (*pros ton theon*). Unfortunately, we are forced to render a dynamic preposition (*pros*), containing the idea of a movement towards God, by a static 'with'. It is best to express the relationship with a paraphrase: 'The Logos is in the presence of God, turned in loving inseparable communion towards God — and God is turned equally towards him.' This union is outside time (John deliberately uses the timeless 'was' here), and is so close that John can say: 'And Godly was the Word.' We must be careful not to take this as an identification of two persons in one. That sort of thinking came at a later stage. All the Greek wants to tell us is that the closeness of these two was such that they became one. As the New English Bible translates beautifully: 'And what God was, the Word was.' We are dealing with a closeness which led to an identity. We are familiar with the closeness which human love can generate. It is uncanny, when two people are so very much in love that they can sense the feelings and reactions of the other — can read clearly the way the loved one will react — and can feel so very deeply the pain of that all-important 'other'. This is an experienced *reality* at the human level. It is this same reality in God which can enable John to cry out: 'And what God was, the Word was.' This Word, which will be spoken to men in the person of Jesus Christ, in none other than the fulness of God himself, to whom the Son is united in the closest of all bonds of love:

'Believe me, that I am in the Father and the Father in me' (14.11).

'*He* was in the beginning with (!) God.' Even though we are still contemplating the life of the Word in God, the reader (to whom the Prologue is addressed) knows to whom the Logos refers, and John stresses that fact by his emphatic repetition — all that has been said applies to *the man* whom they believe to be the Logos.

(b) The Word's revealing role as the light of men (vv. 3-4)

> 'All has happened through him and without him nothing took place. What took place in him was life and the life was the light of men.'

Having meditated on the reality of the relationship that exists between God and his Word from all time, the Prologue now makes a sharp break, going outwards from the mystery of the life of God into the sphere of salvation: 'All has happened through him.' Most translations will give 'all things were made through him'. The verb in question (*ginomai*) can have both meanings: 'to take place' or 'to be made'.[8] Generally scholars and translators take it that John is following Genesis, and now refers to the creation. We think that John is interested in the salvation which has come to us through God's revelation in Jesus Christ, the Word, and this is what 'happened' through him. All that happens is intimately related to the Word, for everything that exists has its sense through him and in him. This is a rather tremendous claim — not just a pious thought about what might possibly be the case, but a clear affirmation of a fact — all things have their very existence, purpose and salvation through and in the Word. Here we are touching on John's answer — the correct answer — to the deep need that is felt in the heart of every man and woman. It was at the centre of the many religions that were flowering in John's world at the end of the first century, especially Gnosticism and the Mystery Religions, and it is at the heart of a great deal of the searchings that are to be found

---

8. Any Greek dictionary will give both meanings: 'to be made, created' and also 'happen, take place'. See especially W. F. Arndt — F. W. Gingrich, *A Greek-English Lexicon of the New Testament and Other Early Christian Literature* (Chicago, University Press, 1957), pp. 157-158. See T. E. Pollard, 'Cosmology and the Prologue of the Fourth Gospel', *Vigiliae Christianae* 12 (1958), pp. 147-153.

everywhere today. There exists that search to find something which none of us is able to touch ... that desire to go further than where we are at the moment ... that urge to love, to hate, the capacity to cry and to suffer, as well as the capacity to feel the exultation and exhilaration of the spirit which great joy and great love can give to each and every one of us. Why is all this so much a part of us? Here is the Johannine answer: all has happened through him and in him. He is that divine spark which resides within the heart of every man and woman. As John will tell us again later in the Gospel:

'Apart from me you can do nothing' (15.15).

Here one can see the importance of our conviction that the Prologue must be understood as a part of the Gospel as a whole. The Fourth Gospel has little to say on the creation of 'all things', but is entirely concerned with the revelation of 'truth', 'life' and 'light' to all men — found uniquely in Jesus.

There is a question of some importance here which we have already answered by giving you our translation — again very different from some of the usual translations. The original Greek manuscripts had no punctuation, so there are several ways one can read vv. 3-4. The most common ones are:

i. The one we gave:	'All has happened through him, and without him nothing took place. What took place in him was life and the life was the light of men.'
ii. The traditional one:	'And without him was not anything made that was made. In him was life.'

Our understanding of the verb as 'to happen' or 'to take place' leads us to punctuate the verse as above. We must be governed by what the rest of the Gospel says about 'Life'. For the author of this Gospel there is only one source of life: the revelation of God in and through the person of Jesus Christ. As Jesus later proclaims:

'I am the resurrection and the life; he who believes
in me, though he dies, yet shall he live' (11.25).

As this is the case, we feel that in vv. 3-4, John makes two
separate affirmations:

i. All salvation takes place in and through Jesus Christ.
ii. This salvation is then called the 'life' which can en-
    lighten all men.

He is the source of a life that makes sense — he is the
source of the energy arising out of the divine spark which
we described as so central to each one of us. This is the
light of the world. This is the marvel of the incarnation,
and the essence of the Kingdom which Jesus came to establish . . . and it is the light of all mankind, if they will
only turn to it. The light of the divine spark is present in
all of us.

(c) The light of men and the impotency of the darkness (v. 5)

'The light shines in the darkness, and the darkness
has not overcome it.'

There is a discussion of considerable importance behind
the sense of the Greek word which we have translated
'overcome'. Some would like to make this into an intellectual concept and say: 'The light shines in the darkness
and the darkness cannot *comprehend* it.' This is to equate
'the darkness' with the minds of men who are incapable of
grasping the light in an intellectual sense. However, if we
look at the rest of the Gospel, we will find that 'the darkness' is not men. It is the impersonal power of evil (see
8.12; 12.35; 12.46) which is locked in bitter conflict with
Jesus Christ. To the mere historian it will seem that the
darkness wins, and the Cross spells the end of the Light,
but to the man of faith it is paradoxically on the Cross
where the light shines through the darkness: 'When you
have lifted up the Son of Man, then you will know that I
am he' (8.28). It is not that men cannot understand what
the light means, but that the power of evil . . . the power

43

of sin which reigns among men . . . *will not* accept the light. It could, but it *will not*. Despite this, 'the light shines in this immense darkness, but it is not overcome.' There is an essential note of optimism in this passage — the darkness has not overcome the light which is to be found in the person and message of Jesus Christ. The strange Johannine paradox of a glory and a revelation of God (the light) which takes place on a Cross makes its first appearance in this verse.

II — CENTRAL SECTION: The insertion of the Word into the history of salvation (vv. 6-14).

(a) The insertion of the Word into history through the historical witness of John the Baptist to the Light (vv. 6-8)

> 'There was a man sent from God, whose name was John. He came for testimony, to bear witness to the light, that all might believe through him. He was not the light but came to bear witness to the light.'

All of a sudden we are brought down to earth with a bump! We have been moving in the heady heights of Johannine speculation on God and his Word, the Word and salvation, moving outwards from God to us, and then, all of a sudden, we find ourselves in mid-first century Palestine and with a man called John the Baptist.

This has caused many scholars to see these references as secondary, and to leave them out in their study of the Prologue. For Rudolf Bultmann (and others) the Evangelist gives himself away here. The hymn was originally in praise of John the Baptist and now it has been taken over by the followers of Jesus. They have to make these insertions about John the Baptist to keep him, and more specially his followers (see Acts 19), in their place. John the Baptist has to be put into his correct perspective as regards Jesus. There is an important element of truth in that last statement, but the most important role of the reference to the Baptist is to anchor the Prologue in history. It is on purpose that John brings us down from the heady heights of vv. 1-5 suddenly to come to grips with the figure of the Baptist, who is, for John the Evangelist, the supreme witness to the Christ. What the Evangelist says here is not to 'play down' the Baptist — he is 'a man sent from God' and his function is to bear witness to the light. These are honours that no other human being has ever had before — or after. John the Baptist stands astride the two testaments — calling the people from the Old to look now to the New — and to the man who gives sense to the whole of the New Era — Jesus Christ. And we are no longer speculating on God — Christ and the World, but we are dealing with concrete historical facts. The Prologue is no longer concerned with God, his Word and its revealing task as the light of men. Now we are among men as John the Baptist, an identifiable historical character, bears witness to the Light, performing a task which recalls the words of second Isaiah: 'Arise, shine, for your Light has come, and the glory of the Lord has risen upon you, for behold, darkness shall cover the earth, and thick blackness the peoples; but the Lord will rise upon you . . . and nations shall come to your light" (Is 60.1-2).

(b) The Light which comes into the world (v. 9)

> 'The true light that enlightens every man was coming into the world.'

As we see the Prologue unfolding a series of themes repeated over and over again, we have no difficulty in recognising the reference to the incarnation here. It is 'the true light' who was coming into the world. The Light is 'true' in the biblical sense of that word: it is the uniquely genuine, authentic and perfect revelation of God to the world. This theme is acted out dramatically later in the Gospel, in the experience of the man born blind (ch. 9).

(c) The dual reply of men:

- negative (vv. 10-11)
- positive (vv. 12-13)

'He was in the world, and the world was made through him, yet the world knew him not. He came to his own home, and his own people received him not. But to all who received him, who believed in his name, he gave power to become children of God; who were born, not of blood, nor of the will of the flesh, nor of the will of man, but of God.'

We have seen (vv. 1-2) 'The Word with God' and then in vv. 3-5 'The Word and Salvation'. Now we go one step further; John is no longer concerned with the whole of Creation, but with men: the word and its relationship to the community of mankind.

Recalling the fact that all has its sense and existence in and through him, John turns to see what happened when that all-creating Word broke into that creation. There is a word in the Book of Wisdom which speaks beautifully of the reality that we are about to consider. Although originally a reflection on the last 'plague' before the Exodus (see Exod 11.4-9; 12.29-32), it may have been in John's mind as he reflected on the mystery of the Incarnation and man's refusal to accept it:

'For while gentle silence enveloped all things,
and night in its swift course was now half gone,
thy all powerful word leaped from heaven,
from the royal throne,
into the midst of a land that was doomed,
a stern warrior carrying the sharp sword
of thy authentic command,
and touched heaven while standing on the earth'
(Wisdom 18.14-16).

It is important to recall, at this stage, what we said about the 'Word', and the purpose of that 'Word's' becoming flesh. It was he who 'was' from all time who now 'leaps down' in the Incarnation to become one of us:

'No one has gone up to heaven, to receive the revelation of God — but someone has come down —

the Son of Man!
And as Moses lifted up the snake in the desert, so
must that Son of Man be lifted up, so that all who
believe in Him might have life eternal'

(see 3:13-15).

But here is the problem — 'all who believe in Him'. This
Word is the unique communication of God with us, but
how have we reacted?

John pens this part of the Prologue with the life and
death of Jesus in mind — Jesus did come to 'his own
home' — and his own people rejected him and nailed him
on a cross. Strangely enough, it was through the cross that
Jesus was to show the glory of God — and 'They shall look
on him whom they have pierced' (19.37). Those who have
accepted him — who have believed in his name — have
been given the power to become children of God. How
carefully phrased that is! Belief in Christ gives us the
power to become the Sons of God. It will be within our
grasp. We all exist in and through Jesus. It is because of
this that we are able to *know* and *feel* that there is something integral to our very being which is untouchable,
unutterable, but which can only be worked out by a living
of life in its fulness. This is the concrete evidence of the
'divine spark' which rules and makes sense out of our lives
as human beings. And all this was so because 'All has
happened through him, and without him nothing took
place' (v. 3). Now, because that Word has come into the
world, we have the ability to come to understand the
reason why we can love and be loved etc. ... because that
divine spark is not just a vague 'something' which will ever
remain a mystery to us — but it can be fully understood
and seen as the concrete evidence that our ultimate sense
is found in our being 'children of God' — and not mere
products of human flesh, desire or will.[9]

9. Since the time of the early Fathers (especially Ter-
tullian) there has been discussion about a possible reference to
the virgin birth in Jn 1.13. We need not consider the matter
here. It would be a possible interpretation if one accepted the

(d) The gift of the incarnate Son — a free gift which is truth
(v. 14)

> 'The Word became flesh and dwelt among us, the
> fulness of a gift which is truth: we have beheld his
> glory, glory as of the only Son from the Father.'

Far too often this verse is taken to be the most important
and unique statement in the whole Gospel. This is to lose
a great deal of the message of the Prologue. It fits in here
as the logical consequence of what has gone before and
what will follow. It is not here that John mentions the
Incarnation for the first time — it was mentioned in v. 9:
'The true light that enlightens every man was coming into
the world', and could even be the point of v. 5: 'The light
shines in the darkness, and the darkness has not overcome
it', while the very choice of the title 'Logos' for v. 1
already indicates that the Prologue is concerned with
God-Man *communication*.

John now makes his point crystal-clear: God has
spoken to the world — and his Word has become flesh.
This presence of God among men in the person of Jesus
Christ is not to be used as our classical passage to prove
the divinity of Christ in our books of Dogmatic Theology.
Of course, it can do that for us — but this was not even a
problem for John. He is more concerned to tell us that
here — in the person of Jesus Christ, the Word who has
become one of us — we can find the answer to the profound drives to love and to exist in love that God has
planted in the heart and soul of each one of us at creation.
Thus the most important part of the verse is not the clear
statement that the Word became flesh — but the con-

---

singular reading 'who was born' (*egennethe* instead of
egennethesan) found only in a few manuscripts. The evidence,
at best, is slender. However, one should see on this question,
R. E. Brown, *John*, pp. 11-12; J. Galot, *Etre ne de Dieu: Jean
1.13*, Analecta Biblica 37 (Rome, Pontifical Biblical Institute,
1969); J. McHugh, *The Mother of Jesus in the New Testament*
(London, Darton, Longman and Todd, 1975), pp. 255-268.

sequences of that Incarnation: that this man, Jesus Christ, who was the Word made flesh, was the fulness of a gift which is the ultimate truth. Our translations usually read: 'full of grace and truth'. The Greek word for 'grace' (*charis*) has become 'grace' from its use in Paul. We must be careful not to read Paul into John. A study of the word *charis* in biblical and extra-biblical material shows that it can also have the meaning of 'gift'.[10] There is a further Greek use of our word 'and' which does *not* indicate an accumulation of different ideas but where the second noun explains the first.[11] Thus in our case we have the translation 'the fulness of a gift of truth', i.e., a gift which is truth. The incarnation, hinted at in vv. 1 and 5 and announced in v. 9 is explained in v. 14. The Word is now available to the senses of men. In beholding the incarnate word, dwelling among us, the 'glory of the only Son' can be *seen*. Using a term taken from the Greek version of the Old Testament to refer to God's *visible* presence among his people (*doxa* = glory), John claims that in Jesus the abiding presence of God can be seen. God is revealed in a unique way, and this revelation is described as 'the fulness of a gift which is truth'. What this means will be explained further in vv. 16-18.

III — CONCLUSION: The revealing role of the Word, Jesus Christ, in the history of all of us who believe (vv. 15-18)

(a) The activity of the Baptist among men, witnessing to the pre-existent Word (v. 15)

John bore witness to him, and cried, 'This was he of whom I said, "He who comes after me ranks before me, for he was before me." '

---

10. See S. A. Panimolle, *Il Dono della Legge*, pp. 297-319.

11. See F. Blass — A. Debrunner — R. W. Funk, *A Greek Grammar of the New Testament and Other Early Christian Literature* (Chicago, Chicago University Press, 1961), para. 442,16.

In vv. 6-8 there was a third person report on the Baptist, but here he is actively present among men, proclaiming the secondary nature of his role, because of the pre-existence of the Logos.

John the Baptist is the witness who recalls for us what was solemnly announced about the Logos in vv. 1-2. Now it is no longer a speculation about the Word in God, but the witness of a man about this same Word among men.

(c) The gift of God to all of us (v. 16)
   'And from his fulness we have all received, a gift in
   place of a gift.'

The conclusion of the Prologue is closer to our personal history. John reaffirms that it is from the Word that *we* can receive all things, that he in whom we exist can give us of his fulness. Our translations usually describe that fulness as 'grace upon grace', conveying an idea of an overflowing superabundance, but this is not what the Greek really says, nor does it appear to us to be what John would say. As we have already seen, Paul is the writer who most uses the term *charis* to mean 'grace' in the sense in which we speak about grace today. Translators are influenced by Paul's use of the term, and apply that meaning to the word in the Prologue — the only place in the Fourth Gospel where the word is used. The Greek word can also mean 'a gift'. Here we are dealing with two gifts, and they are separated by a preposition which is also badly translated — *anti*. It really means 'in place of'. If we translate the Greek as it stands, we have John telling us that we have received from the fulness of the Word 'a gift in place of a gift'. What that means is then explained in v. 17.

(d) The concrete gift of Jesus Christ in relation to the gift of the Law — Jesus Christ as a free gift which is the truth (vv. 17-18)

   'For the Law was given through Moses, the gift of
   the truth came through Jesus Christ. No one has

ever seen God; the only Son, turned towards the
Father, he has made him known.'

V. 17 explains what was said in v. 16. The use of 'was
given' indicates that the Law of Moses was a gift — but
this has been replaced by the gift of the Truth: an event
which has 'happened' (the verb *ginomai* is used again)
through the mediation of Jesus Christ. What has been
suggested throughout the Prologue is now confirmed. The
Logos is identified, for the first time, with Jesus Christ.
Once the Logos is described as having taken flesh, John
speaks of Jesus Christ. As this is the case, all that has been
said of the Johannine Logos can now be called Johannine
Christology.

The concluding verse shows again why the revelation of
the Logos, Jesus Christ, is Truth. This must be understood
in the light of some currents of Jewish piety. It was
commonly believed that the great saints of Israel
(Abraham, Moses, Enoch, Isaiah) had ascended to God to
receive their knowledge of him, so that they could
descend again to reveal to mankind what they had seen.
John cuts across this speculation by announcing, with
vigour, that *no-one* (the Greek word *oudeis* is emphatic)
has ever seen God (see 3.13). There is *only one* (again a
Greek emphatic *ekeinos* is used), the only Son,[12] who has
revealed God with an ultimate authority.

Our translations here normally explain that the only
Son is able to make the Father known because he 'is in the
bosom of the Father'. This is usually taken to refer to
the glorified Jesus' presence with his Father — a sort of
primitive reference to what became the later theology of
the Trinity. However, the Greek word translated by
'bosom' (*kolpos*) could never indicate a place of "indwel-

---

12. There are good witnesses which read 'the only God'
instead of 'the only Son'. For a discussion of this, see B. M.
Metzger, *A Textual Commentary on the Greek New Testament*
(London-New York, United Bible Society, 1971), p. 198. The
added note by A. Wikgren on that page stands behind our
decision to read 'the only Son'.

ling". It means 'chest' — the external part of the body. Our nuances of 'indwelling' here have come to us from the Latin Vulgate's necessary use of 'in sinu' to translate the Greek *eis kolpon*. The Latin word *sinus* (like the French 'sein' or the Italian "seno") has a double meaning: the breast (external) and also the womb (internal). Because of the possibilities of the second meaning, the whole phrase is normally understood as a reference to the co-existence of the Father and the Son after the glorification of Jesus. We suggest that it refers to the historical, incarnate Jesus. This explains the translation which we gave above: 'turned towards the Father'. Taking up v. 1, with which it forms an 'inclusion', it repeats the same idea of dynamic 'movement towards' the Father which was involved in the preposition *pros* in v. 1, and is repeated with the preposition *eis* here. This latter preposition does not normally express a state of 'dwelling'; it involves some sort of movement (although, it must be said, by the time of the New Testament some of these Greek prepositions had lost their full force). If the Evangelist wished to speak of Jesus' life 'in' the Father, why did he not use the preposition 'in', rather than 'towards'? We are told here of Jesus' loving complementary union of purpose and will with the Father, even in his earthly ministry. Again, this interpretation is but the first indication of a theme which is to become central in the Gospel, where the historical Jesus insists upon his continual union with God his Father (see passim, but especially 5.19-30). In this way, the Prologue concludes by repeating, in an inclusion with v. 1, what has been said in the opening verses. However, there is a very important progression, as now the pre-existent divine Logos, the medium of all salvation through his unique role as revealer and revelation itself (vv. 1-5), is incarnate, but he maintains his union with the Father, thus maintaining his role as the unique bearer of the saving revelation of God.

5. *Conclusion*

John calls Jesus "the Logos" when he wishes to speak of his

pre-existing with God, before all time. In the beginning, when everything else came into existence, the Logos already "was" (1.1). The title appears only four times in the whole Gospel — always in the Prologue (three times in v. 1 and once in v. 14). The *reader* is given the key to the mystery of Jesus in the very first verse of the book. This mystery, however, is never fully grasped by the characters who 'see' Jesus, because they never understand that he has pre-existed with God as the very Word of God himself. As T. W. Manson has written: 'The Jewish interlocutors get at cross-purposes with the Johannine Christ because they think they are holding a debate with Jesus the son of Joseph from Nazareth, whereas they are really listening to the incarnate word of God.'[13] But we, the readers, know who Jesus is. We know of his origins because we have read the Prologue.

Within these verses, however, 'the Logos' is used exclusively to speak of Jesus' presence outside history. Once we are told that the Logos became flesh (v. 14), the titles change. Now he is called 'the only Son from the Father' (v. 14), 'Jesus Christ' (v. 17) and 'the only Son' (v. 18). This appears to be important. As we have seen, it is often argued that the limitation of this title to the Prologue is an indication that John found a Logos-hymn already composed, and added it to his Gospel. We suggest that the use of "Logos" to speak *exclusively* of the pre-existence of Jesus was not simply imposed upon John by his sources, but that it was a deliberate choice of the Evangelist. The Jesus of the Fourth Gospel cannot be understood unless one accepts his pre-existence with the Father whom he claims to reveal to mankind. Despite the importance of this fact, *only* in the Prologue is his pre-existence explicitly taught. Thus, only in the Prologue is Jesus called 'the Logos'.

---

13. T. W. Manson — M. Black (ed.), *On Paul and John*, Studies in Biblical Theology 38 (London, SCM Press, 1963), pp. 158-159.

Chapter 3

THE SON OF GOD[1]

One only has to read through the Fourth Gospel to come to the conclusion that the Evangelist works out the story of the life, death and resurrection of Jesus of Nazareth from the presupposition that this man was 'the Son of God'. Jesus' being 'Son' and 'Son of God' is so important for John that one could understandably conclude that he wants to tell us about Jesus' nature — his divine Sonship. There is a danger that we might see a description of Jesus as a divine being in the title, and classical theological manuals generally use the Fourth Gospel to find their 'proof texts' for the divinity of Jesus. A careful examination of John's description of Jesus as the Son of God, however, shows that John was not primarily interested in Jesus' nature.

An outstanding German scholar, Ernst Käsemann, has recently written a book in which he claims that the Johannine Jesus is 'God going about on earth', and that he cannot be understood as a real man.[2] This is the overstatement of what has traditionally been taught in our theological manuals. According to Käsemann, the incarnation mentioned in the Prologue (1.14) should not be stressed, as the real point of these verses is to announce Jesus as a divine epiphany.[3] He does not need food, knows everything, and performs the most miraculous wonders. All of this points to a sort of naive docetism, in the sense of a docetism which is only on the way

---

1. On this topic, see F. J. Moloney, 'The Johannine Son of God', *Salesianum* 38 (1976), pp. 71-86. I have adapted and simplified that article for the following chapter.

2. E. Käsemann, *The Testament of Jesus. A Study of the Gospel of John in the Light of Chapter 17* (London, SCM Press, 1968).

3. See also E. Käsemann, 'The Structure and Purpose of the Prologue to John's Gospel', in *New Testament Questions of Today* (London, SCM Press, 1969), pp. 138-167.

to its fullest expression. God did not become a man, but he only changed his place from heaven to earth for a while, and appeared in human form in order to communicate with us. 'He does not really change himself, but only his place. Human fate is thrust upon him so that in a divine manner he may endure it and overcome it.'[4]

It appears to us that both the metaphysical and docetic interpretation of the Johannine Son of God miss the point of John's use of the title. The Son of God title is continually used in contexts dealing with the salvation of men, which is at once the will of God (the Father) and the task of the Son. This salvation is possible because the relationship between Jesus and his Father reaches outside the limitations of time, but it takes place in and through the *incarnate* Son — Jesus of Nazareth. The concluding verse of the Gospel (20.31) already gives the lie to any effort to abstract about the nature of Jesus' being: John wrote his Gospel so that people might believe in *Jesus* as the Son of God, and thus come to eternal life. This message is addressed to men and women living in history, and John himself tells us that some of them could not see past the human Jesus (see 7.24; 8.15). It is important for us to understand that the recognition and confession of Jesus as the Son of God can only happen in the human sphere. John is convinced that it does happen that way. He deliberately chose to write a Gospel — to tell the story of Jesus of Nazareth — to show that God revealed himself through his Son, especially in the glory which shines through the Son's performance of the task given to him by the Father (1.14; 2.11; 5.44; 11.4; 11.40; 12.41 and especially 17.1-5), and finally in the enigma of the Cross (see especially 19.28-30,37).

The importance of the use of 'the Son' can be seen from a mere material comparison with the rest of the New Testament. The absolute use of the term appears only three times in the Synoptic Gospels (Matt 11.27 par. Lk 10.22; Mk 13.32 par. Matt 24.36; Matt 28.19), once in Paul (I Cor 15.28) and five times in Hebrews (Heb 1.2,8; 3.6; 5.8; 7.28). In the Fourth

---

4. E. Käsemann, *The Testament of Jesus*, p. 12.

Gospel Jesus speaks of his Sonship twenty times (Jn 3.16,17,18; 5.19-twice, 20,21,22,23-twice, 25,26; 6.40; 8.35-36; 10.36; 11.4; 14.13; 17.1-twice); four times it is a Johannine comment (3.35,36-twice; 20.31); it appears once in in the Prologue (1.18) and four times on the lips of others (1.34: John the Baptist; 1.49: Nathanael; 11.27: Martha; 19.7: the Jews). Besides the sayings which explicitly mention Jesus' Sonship, there is a further series of sayings in which Jesus refers to God as his Father. As well as repeating many of the notions also found in the Son (of God) sayings, they fill out our understanding of the importance, for John, of the relationship between Jesus and God, whom he can call his Father.

The Johannine Son (of God) sayings nearly always express a direct relationship between God and Jesus, the Father and the Son. This is generally shown by the fact that it is precisely this relationship which is being proclaimed by Jesus (3.16,18; 5.19-26; 6.40; 10.36; 11.4; 14.13; 17.1), by the Evangelist (1.18; 3.35), by John the Baptist (1.34), or refused by the Jews (the attitude which gave rise to ch. 5; 19.7). If Jesus is to call God his Father, then his Sonship will be expressed in terms of that relationship. It is important to notice, however, that this relationship is never shown as a static privilege: the Son was sent by the Father to bring life to all those who believe in him (3.16). The whole point of Jesus' being the Son of God is that he may bring salvation to man by revealing God to them. From the lists given above it can be seen that there are two passages in the Gospel where one finds a heavy concentration on the title, 'the Son (of God)': 3.16-21 and 5.19-26. A closer look at these passages should indicate whether or not our claim that Jesus' Sonship is not a static privilege, but an indication of his task to reveal the Father, is true.

1. *John 3.16-21*

The passage 3.16-21 is a section of a mini-discourse of Jesus, found in the complex literary composition of 2.23-3.36. In a general division of the Gospel, the second part of the Book of Signs runs from 2.1-4.54: from Cana to

Cana. As we indicated in our first chapter, the theme of this section is a question of the correct type of faith. This theme is indicated by John's comments in 2.23-25. Editorial comments are vital indications of what the Evangelist wants his readers to understand. Here he states: 'Now when he was in Jerusalem at the Passover feast, many believed in his name when they saw the signs which he did; but Jesus did not trust himself to them, because he knew all men and needed no one to bear witness of man; for he himself knew what was in man' (2.23-25). After this statement of the theme, John continues his narrative. He links Nicodemus with what has been said in the introduction by playing on the word 'man' — 'Now there was a man of the Pharisees . . .' The chapter then unfolds as two examples of faith in Jesus, and two reflections upon these examples. Thus this section of the 'Cana to Cana' series develops in the following fashion:

I — 2.23-25: The question of the correct type of faith.

II — 3.1-10: The first example, Nicodemus, fails to go beyond the limitations of his traditional Jewish faith. He has not correctly understood nor believed in Jesus.

III — 3.11-21: Jesus reflects on this in a short discourse.

vv. 11-15: Jesus, the Son of Man, is the revealer of the heavenly things.

vv. 16-21: The salvation-condemnation brought by the revelation of the Son who has come into the world.

IV — 3.22-30: The second example, John the Baptist, understands the role of Jesus as the revealer from heaven, and sees his own role in the light of that understanding.

V — 3.31-36: The Evangelist reflects on this:

vv. 31-34: Jesus, 'he who comes from heaven', is the revealer of 'the words of God'.

vv. 35-36: The salvation-condemnation brought by the revelation of the Son who has come into the world.

From the above general indication of the themes involved, it can be seen that vv. 11-21 are paralleled by vv.
31-36. A closer reading of these two 'reflections' on the
faith of the two examples (Nicodemus and John the
Baptist) shows a deliberate repetition of the same ideas.
Two closely linked themes stand out: the revelation
brought by Jesus (see vv. 11-15 = vv. 31-34) and the
consequent possibility of salvation or condemnation which
flows from man's response to this revelation (see vv. 16-21
= vv. 35-36). In other words, the discourse firstly indicates
the *fact* of the revelation of God which can be found in
Jesus, and then turns to tell man that he can be saved or
lost according to his acceptance or refusal of that revelation. When the consequences of this revelation for our
salvation are clearly spelt out (vv. 16-21 and vv. 35-36),
Jesus is continually referred to as 'the Son' (vv. 16, 17, 18,
35, 36). The purpose of Jesus' mission is explained in terms
of the initiative of the Father-God. God has so loved the
world that he sent his only Son (v. 16) in order that the
world may have the opportunity of accepting or refusing
the light and the truth (vv. 19-21, 35-36) which are to be
found in him (vv. 18 and 36), and thus come to salvation or
condemnation (vv. 17 and 36). The choice of the title 'the
Son (of God)' seems to be deliberately linked to those parts
of the discourse which refer to the salvific consequences of
the incarnation.

2. *John 5.19-30*

This is made even clearer in 5.19-26, where one might
expect a great concentration on what may be called the
more static nature of the union between the Father and the
Son. After healing a man at the pool of Bethesda on the
Sabbath, the authority of Jesus is questioned by his
opponents (5.9b-18). Jesus replies to them by going
beyond the legal questions which they are asking, and by
pointing to his absolute union of dependence upon the
Father-God. The key to the reply of Jesus is already
found in v. 17: 'My Father is working still and I am work-

ing'. This statement, in the context of a conflict over the observance of the Sabbath, has to be understood in the light of Jewish theology. It was clear to the Jews that God could not rest on the Sabbath, but this caused them serious theological difficulties. On the one hand the Torah taught clearly that God rested on the Sabbath (see Gen 2.2; Exod 20.11; 31.17), yet on the other hand the faith of Israel preserved the belief that God never left the world to follow its own destiny. God always directed history, and especially the history of his chosen people. Life goes on: children are born on the Sabbath, people die on the Sabbath; God must be always giving life and judging. He could not possibly cease to be active on the Sabbath, or else history would come to an end. He must therefore be 'working still' on the Sabbath — but *only* God could be allowed this prerogative. Yet Jesus included himself under the rubric of his Father who works on the Sabbath — 'and I am working'. This is *correctly* understood by the Jews (v. 18) and they regard his claim as a blasphemy of the highest order (see Gen 3.5; Is 14.4; Ezek 28; Dan 11.31-36; 2 Macc 9.12). Here, more than anywhere else in the Gospel, does John have to prove that Jesus *is* the Son of God, and one could expect a heavy concentration on the *nature* of Jesus' Sonship, in order to show that Jesus had every right to make his claim: 'My Father is working still and I am working' (v. 17).

In fact, the first part of the discourse (vv. 19-30) is devoted to an explanation of Jesus' absolute dependence upon his Father. The rest of the discourse (vv. 31-47) deals with the validity (truth) of the unique witness which he brings, a consequence of the union between the Father and the Son explained in vv. 19-30.

The section of the discourse with which we are concerned is worked out between two verses which state the theme of the whole passage and act as an inclusion:

v. 19	v. 30
'The Son can do nothing of his own accord'.	'I can do nothing of my own accord'.

Between these two statements, the discourse unfolds in the following fashion:

vv. 19-20: The absolute dependence of the Son upon the Father.

v. 21: The *exercising* of the Son's authority to give life.

v. 22: The *basis* of the Son's authority to judge.

v. 23: The honour due to the Son because of his relationship with the Father.

vv. 24-25: The Son as the life-giver, with judgment as a sub-theme.

v. 26: The *basis* of the Son's authority to give life.

v. 27: The *exercising* of the Son's authority to judge, as Son of Man.

vv. 28-29: The Son as judge, with life-giving as a sub-theme.

v. 30: The absolute dependence of Jesus upon the Father.

Jesus can only win his case if he shows his opponents that he is one with God, who alone could judge and give life on the Sabbath. Thus, the passage is concerned with the demonstration of the total dependence of the Son upon the Father (vv. 19-22, 26, 30), but it is a dependence which leads to a certain equality, where the honour which is due to the Father is due also to the Son (v. 23). As the passage is concerned with the vindication of Jesus' authority, he *must* turn back to the Father, who gives sense and purpose to his existence. However, it is not allowed to rest there, as Jesus again speaks clearly of the consequence of his oneness with the Father. Because of this oneness the Son is also the life-giver and the judge. He who is open to the word (revelation) of the Son already has eternal life (vv. 24-25) and thus the revealer also brings judgment, as men accept or refuse the revelation, and judge themselves (vv. 27-29). Thus, even in this context, where it is imperative for John to show that Jesus is the Son of God to avoid a justifiable charge of blasphemy, Jesus' role as life-giver and judge eventually becomes the dominant theme, and any consideration of Jesus' nature as the Son of God remains secondary.

3. *Further Son of God Sayings*

Other sayings, spread through the Gospel, argue the same case. John the Baptist's role in the Fourth Gospel is always to point to the true meaning and purpose of Jesus' person and mission. The Fourth Gospel is the only Gospel which speaks of the Baptist as 'sent from God' (1.6) and he is used throughout the Gospel to point the way to Jesus (1.6-8, 15,19-34; 3.22-30). In the section of the Gospel which discusses the various types of faith (2.1-4.54), John the Baptist is presented as an example of the correct attitude to Jesus (3.22-30). He recognises the origin of Jesus' revelation (3.27), he accepts it (3.29) and understands his own role in the light of the ultimate significance of Jesus (3.30). Given the important part which the Baptist plays in this Gospel, the confession of 1.34 must be seen as a valid proclamation of the identity of Jesus, in reply to a series of guesses from others. The Baptist continually points away from himself towards Jesus, and concludes his introduction to Jesus by calling him the Lamb of God and the Son of God. The association of the two titles is important. While the precise meaning of the title 'the Lamb of God' is difficult to determine, the important aspect for our purposes is that the Lamb of God 'takes away the sin of the world' (1.29). Here John expresses in negative terms what he generally calls the giving of life. Thus Jesus is again presented as the Son of God in a context which deals with the salvation which he brings to men. It is important to notice that this is the concluding title used by the Baptist, and should be understood as the high point and climax of his witness to Jesus. Thus, the functions of Jesus as the one who 'takes away the sin of the world' (v. 29) and who 'baptizes with the Holy Spirit' (v. 33) are involved in the

Baptist's confession of him as 'the Son of God'.

True freedom could come to the Jews if they would accept the revelation ('my words': 8.37) brought by the Son from his Father (8.34-38): 'If the Son makes you free, you will be free indeed' (8.36). However, the Jews have set themselves against him. In Jesus' encounter with the Jews in the second half of ch. 8 (vv. 31-59) he twice offers them the truth and life which could set them free, under the sole condition that they accept the revelation which the Son brings:

vv. 31-32: 'If you continue in my word, you are truly my disciples and you will know the truth and the truth will make you free.'

v. 51: 'If anyone keeps my word, he will never see death.'

The Jews fail to meet this condition by refusing to accept Jesus' words on both occasions:

v. 33: 'We are descendents of Abraham, and have never been in bondage to anyone. How is it that you say, "You will be made free?" '

v. 52: 'Now we know that you have a demon. Abraham died, as did the prophets; and you say "If anyone keeps my word he will never taste death." Are you greater than our Father Abraham who died?'

Notice how the Jews take up and repeat the 'words' of Jesus himself, throwing them back at him in their refusal to accept his revelation of the truth. They will not admit his origin and his relationship with the Father, announced in vv. 34-38 in terms of Jesus' Sonship. They accuse him of blasphemy because of this claim (this is the significance of the attempted stoning in 8.59; see also 10.36), and in the end they reject him totally and crucify him 'because he has made himself the Son of God' (19.7). In their failure to see and believe in Jesus as the Son of God they turned their backs on the gift of life offered by the Father, through his Son: 'For this is the will of my Father, that everyone who sees the Son and believes in him should have eternal life' (6.40).

4. *Unsatisfactory uses of 'the Son of God'*

Not every use of the title 'the Son of God' is seen as satisfactory by the Fourth Evangelist. In 1.49 Nathanael, after being told that he had been under a fig tree before he was called by Philip (1.48), confesses: 'Rabbi, you are the Son of God, you are the King of Israel' (1.49). One must notice that Jesus *corrects* this confession in terms of 'greater things' which he (and others, as the 'you' is plural in v. 50) would 'see' — in the Son of Man. Nathanael's profession of faith in Jesus is to be understood in the light of Jewish messianic expectations (see 2 Sam 7.14; Ps 2.7), and the title 'the Son of God' remains a term for a messianic figure, paralleled by 'Rabbi' and 'the King of Israel'. Jesus' reply, in terms of the future revelation ('will see') of the Son of Man, shows that Nathanael's confession was not sufficient. He is still blocked off from a true understanding of Jesus, as he uses titles which are understandable to him and his world.

In 11.27 Martha professes faith in Jesus as 'the Christ, the Son of God, he who is coming into the world'. We are again dealing with Jewish messianic hopes. Objectively speaking, Jesus was the Christ, the Son of God and 'the coming one',[5] but the whole context of lack of faith warns us that, for John, she has not understood what that meant. The Christ and 'the coming one' can both be quite easily understood as titles within the context of Jewish messianic

---

5. For an up-to-date study which shows that this term 'the coming one' (*ho erchomenos*) was, in fact, a messianic title, see E. Arens, *The Elthon-Sayings in the Synoptic Tradition. A Historico-Critical Investigation*, Orbis Biblicus et Orientalis 10 (Fribourg, Universitatsverlag; Gottingen, Vandenhoeck and Ruprecht, 1976), pp. 288-300.

hopes, which John continually corrects (see especially 6.14-15, where 'the coming one' is also used). So it is also with 'the Son of God' in this case. That Martha is thinking in terms which she herself understands, rather than the Johannine idea of Jesus as 'the Son of God' can be seen from the very next verse (v. 28) where Jesus is described as 'the teacher': 'the teacher is here'. This term was used by Nicodemus (3.2), but it was corrected by Jesus in terms of 'the Son of Man' and 'the Son of God' (see 3.11-21). Her lack of true faith is shown later in the incident when she queries Jesus' authority in v. 39.

These two insufficient uses of 'the Son of God' by Nathanael and Martha warn us that we must interpret the title within the dynamic of Johannine thought as it develops in each context. The very fact that the title may be used incorrectly in the context of Jewish messianic expectations throws into even greater relief the significance of the *Johannine* use of the term. For John the title demands a recognition of something far more than the identification of Jesus with the Jewish messiah. It refers to his origin from God and his working in a continual union of love with God, his Father, whom he reveals. If this is not understood by the person who confesses Jesus as the Son of God, then that confession must be unsatisfactory.

So far we have been concerned with some major moments in the Fourth Gospel when Jesus' mission as the Son of God has clearly been shown as his mission to reveal his Father to men, so that they might be saved, or to use John's terms, set free and given life. Throughout the Gospel Jesus' authority to reveal his Father is shown to lie in the fact that he is 'from' the Father: 'We have beheld his glory as of the only Son from the Father' (1.14; see also 7.29; 8.42, 9.33; 12.5; 15.26; 16.27).[6] In other words, he is able to reveal the Father because he has pre-existed with the Father.

---

6. See, on this point, C. H. Dodd, *The Interpretation of the Fourth Gospel*, pp. 259-260.

5. *The glorification of the Son of God*

On two occasions Jesus speaks of the glory of the Son of God. He foretells that Lazarus' illness is not unto death; 'It is for the glory of God, so that the Son of God may be glorified by means of it' (11.4). Two points are made in these words. Firstly the glory of God is revealed in the event of the miracle (v. 4b and v. 40). This has also been said of Jesus' first miracle, at Cana (see 2.11). The second point, which interests us here, is made in the promise that the Son of God would be glorified by means of the miracle. To understand this statement properly we must remember that the Lazarus miracle is the event which triggers off the final decision that Jesus must die (11.47-53; see also 12.9-11). The Son of God will be glorified because of the miracle. What this means cannot be fully understood without the help of the other saying which speaks about the glorification of the Son of God. At the beginning of his parting prayer, Jesus turns to his Father and prays: 'Father, the hour has come; glorify thy Son that the Son may glorify thee . . . and now, Father, glorify thou me in thy own presence with the glory which I had with thee before the world was made' (17.1,5). It is clear that Jesus is speaking of the glory which will be his when he returns to the presence of his Father, the glory which was his before the world was made (1.1-2,14). However, 17.1 tells us that this will come about through 'the hour' which is now at hand. As we shall see later, the 'hour' is Jesus' 'passing over' through his being lifted up on the Cross, and returning to the Father (see especially 13.1). Only now is 11.4c clear. The Lazarus miracle triggers off 'the hour' by means of which the Son of God is glorified. In fact, the phrase which we have translated as 'by means of it' could have a deeper meaning. The Greek (*di ' autes*) probably refers to the Passion, *through which* Jesus must pass in order to go to the Father. This reflects the idea of 'movement through' the Cross, reflected in 13.1, where John tells us that 'Jesus knew that his hour had come to depart *out of* this word *to* the Father.'

6. *The Johannine Son of God*

The exalted claims of Jesus, that he is the Son of God and that because of his Sonship he has authority to reveal what he has seen with the Father and thus bring eternal life to those who believe in him, is a strange message indeed. It can only be understood in the light of the Prologue, where one is provided with the key to the mystery.[7] The last verses of the Prologue (vv. 17-18) are concerned with an explanation of the whole passage in terms of the gift of Jesus Christ, over against the gift of the Law of Moses. In v. 17 the pre-existent Logos is identified, for the first time, with Jesus Christ, and the passage concludes by referring to Jesus in the following terms: 'No one has ever seen God; the only Son, who is turned in loving union with the Father, he has made him known.' To do this, the pre-existent Son, whom John has called the Logos, became flesh and dwelt among us, revealing the truth, and displaying a glory in his human state 'as of the only Son from the Father' (1.14). Jesus, therefore, is also the pre-existent Son of God who has come into the world to reveal the Father. Thus, it appears that Jesus, the Son of God, is the unique revealer of God because he who was with the Father before the world was made (1.14; 17.5) has authentically revealed his Father before men during his life among them (passim, but especially in 3.16-21, 35-36 and 5.19-30), and will return to his pre-existent glory through 'the hour' (11.4; 17.1.5). At no stage of his presentation of Jesus as

---

7. See M. D. Hooker, 'The Johannine Prologue and the Messianic Secret', pp. 40-52. Prof. Hooker has taken up Lightfoot's suggestion that Mark has a Prologue (Mk 1.1-13) which explains the messianic secret from the first page of his Gospel, and she argues that John is doing exactly the same thing, but in a very different form. See also C. K. Barrett, 'The Prologue of St John's Gospel', 27-29. Barrett, referring to 1.1, has also made the point which we wish to make in *The Gospel according to St. John*, p. 130: 'John intends that the whole of his Gospel shall be read in the light of this verse. The deeds and words of Jesus are the deeds and words of God; if this be not true the book is blasphemous.'

the Son of God has John allowed himself to philosophise about the nature of Jesus' divine Sonship. He is *only* concerned with what that Sonship means for Jesus and, consequently, for mankind.

There has been a great deal of scholarly discussion over the origin of this title of honour for Jesus. It need not detain us here. As we have already seen, John comes at the end of the development of the Gospel traditions. If one must find background for the Johannine use of 'the Son of God', earlier 'Jesus-material', going back, perhaps, to Jesus himself, seems to provide the most satisfactory solution. The famous Johannine thunderbolt, Matt 11.27 par. Lk 10.22, stands very close to the ideas developed by John: 'All things have been delivered to me by my Father; and no one knows the Son except the Father, and no one knows the Father except the Son and anyone to whom the Son chooses to reveal him.' Whether or not this material reports a genuine saying of Jesus need not concern us here, but as it is common to both Matthew and Luke one might suppose that it comes from a source older than both of them (generally called 'Q').[8] There have been several recent suggestions that this saying indicates one of the few facts which we can determine about the self-consciousness of Jesus, i.e. his consciousness of a very special relationship with God, whom he called his Father.[9] There appears to be very little need to look further than the Gospel tradition itself, as the basic idea of John's later development can be found there. As with so many other themes, John has early Christian traditions as his starting point, from which he develops his own unique point of view.

The Johannine Son of God Christology, which we have attempted to outline above, becomes even more explicit

8. See above, p. 11, note 2.

9. This is reflected in the familiar way in which Jesus appears to have addressed God as 'Abba'. See, on this, J. Jeremias, 'Abba', in *The Prayers of Jesus*, Studies in Biblical Theology, Second Series 6 (London, SCM Press, 1967), pp. 11-65.

when one considers the Johannine absolute use of 'the Father'. The Father sends Jesus and gives him his name (17.11,12), his glory (17.22-24), his words (17.8) and his task (5.36; 17.4). The Son replies in perfect union and obedience (3.35; 5.20,30; 8.28,38,40; 10.17-20; 12.50; 15.15; 19.30), knowing that the Father is 'with him' (8.29; 16.20). The Father stands behind the whole of the work and revelatory function of Jesus (12.49; 14.10-11) and, as such, faith and attachment to Jesus means 'belonging' to the Father (14.21,23; 16.26-27). As in the Son of God sayings, we are told that Jesus went out from the Father who sent him, and that he returns to the Father (13.1; 14.12,28; 16.10,27,28; 17.11,13; 20.17) leading the faithful to the place which he has prepared for them (14.2-3; 17.24). From this partial description of some of the themes which are associated with John's use of the term 'Father', it can be seen that the soteriological function which flows from the unique union between the Father and the Son is continued and developed. The oneness which exists between Jesus and Father (10.30; 14.9) means that the Father is revealed in and through Jesus. To accept or refuse Jesus means to accept or refuse the Father (14.10-11). Salvation is offered to men in the revelation of the Father by the Son, Jesus Christ (see especially 14.6; 17.3).

From our brief analysis of Jesus' role as the Son of God in the Fourth Gospel, it can justifiably be concluded that the whole of John's Christology is summarised here. Turned in loving union with God, he has been called the Logos (1.1), but his pre-existent being 'with the Father' is also a part of his being God's Son (1.14; 17.1,5). John also speaks of Jesus' continuing all-important relationship with his Father to give sense to his mission among men (especially 3.16-18 and 5.19-30), and indicates that the Son of God will be finally glorified when he returns again to his Father (17.5). This all-embracing Father-Son relationship, pre-existent, incarnate and resumed in the glorification of the Son through the Cross, has been beautifully described by C. H. Dodd, whose words we would like to make our own:

> The relation of the Father and the Son is an eternal relation, not attained in time, nor ceasing with this life, or with the history of this world. The human career of Jesus is, as it were, a projection of this eternal relation . . . upon the field of time. It is such, not as a mere reflection, or representation of the reality, but in the sense that the love which the Father bore the Son 'before the foundation of the world', and which he perpetually returns, is actively at work in the whole historical life of Jesus. That life displays the unity of Father and Son, in ways which may be described as 'knowledge' or 'indwelling', but as such, not in the sense of withdrawn contemplation, . . . but in the sense that the love of God in Christ creates and conditions an active ministry of word and deed, in which the words are 'spirit and life',[10] and the deeds are 'signs'[10] of the eternal life and light; a ministry which is an aggressive conflict with the powers hostile to life, and ends in a victory of life over death through death. The love of God, thus released in history, brings men into the same unity of which the Father and the Son is the eternal archetype.[11]

---

10. Dodd's original has Greek words here. I have translated them.

11. C. H. Dodd, *Interpretation*, p. 262.

Chapter 4

THE SON OF MAN

1. *The Problem*

At the beginning of this work we claimed that one of the most important contributions made by modern biblical studies to the interpretation of the New Testament, and especially of the Gospels, is an emphasis on the theological rather than historical questions. We insisted, however, that the historical origin of the Christian message must not be lost in the interpreter's search for the original author's or his own 'existential' understanding of the phenomena which lie behind that message. With the exception of Rudolf Bultmann's basically Lutheran insistence on *'sola fide'* (faith alone), most scholars, including Bultmann's own school, would nowadays admit that Christianity must look to Jesus of Nazareth if it is to understand itself.[1]

In any quest for the historical Jesus, the argument ultimately hinges upon what one decides about the Gospel's use of the Christological title 'the Son of Man'. This is the *only* title which is used strictly by Jesus himself to refer to his person, his mission and his destiny. It appears 71 times in the Synoptic tradition (Mark 14 times; Matthew 31 times; Luke 26 times). If we are anxious to know what Jesus thought of himself, his mission and his destiny — the so-called 'self-consciousness' of Jesus — then this looks like the title which should supply the answer. However, the solution is not so near at hand, as there is little agreement on the significance of the title — if it is a title at all! Matthew Black has written: 'The Son of Man problem in the Gospels is one of the most perplexing and

---

1. For a consideration of Bultmann's position and the more recent attempts to return to the historical Jesus, see J. M. Robinson, *A New Quest of the Historical Jesus*, Studies in Biblical Theology 25 (London, SCM Press, 1959).

challenging in the whole field of Biblical theology.'[2] Other scholars are not so optimistic. John Knox complains that the problem is like a jig-saw puzzle in which some of the pieces are missing and others have been altered in the course of transmission, while James Robinson describes the whole discussion among scholars as a 'methodological impasse'.[3] It is beyond our scope to survey this battlefield. We merely wish to sketch the main positions taken by scholars in the debate.

(a) All are authentic sayings of the Lord.[4]

(b) A large group of scholars look to Dan 7 as a scene describing the apocalyptic end of time, and claim that this was the way Jesus used the title which came from Dan 7.13. This theory looks to other intertestamental literature — especially the Book of Enoch and 4 Esdras — to show that Dan 7 and the Son of Man was interpreted in this way at the time of Jesus. Sayings about the suffering Son of Man and the Son of Man among men as the lord of the Sabbath and the forgiver of sins are regarded as creations of the early Church, taking the title from what Jesus said about his final apocalyptic appearance, and widening its use to Jesus among men.[5] This is a very common opinion among German scholars, and the recent work of H. E. Todt has carried this line of thought one step further by claiming that Jesus spoke of *an* apocalyptic Son of

---

2. M. Black, 'The Son of Man in Recent Research and Debate', *The Bulletin of the John Rylands Library* 45 (1963), p. 305.

3. J. Knox, *The Death of Christ* (London, Collins, 1967), p. 87; J. M. Robinson, *A New Quest*, pp. 100-104.

4. Pre-critical scholarship generally assumed this as the case.

5. See, for example, J. Jeremias, *New Testament Theology*, Part One: The Proclamation of Jesus (London, SCM Press, 1971), pp. 257-276.

Man, but did not identify himself with that figure.[6]

(c) Eduard Schweizer will not allow a clearly defined title in the world of Jesus. He argues that Jesus used 'the Son of Man' to refer to himself as the 'present' Son of Man who called all men into question by his use of an enigmatic title.[7]

(d) Some suggest that Jesus *never* used the term. P. Vielhauer has argued that Jesus spoke of the Kingdom of God — never of the Son of Man. Norman Perrin, in his excellent and influential book, *Rediscovering the Teaching of Jesus*, has claimed that the early Christian community explained the resurrection in terms of Dan 7.13, and thus gave birth to the widespread use of the title for Jesus.[8]

(e) Another attempt to solve the problem has come from Geza Vermes, who claims that in Jewish sources the Aramaic '*bar nasha*' was only a circumlocution for 'I'. The phrase 'the Son of Man' has no theological content, and is not to be linked with Dan 7.13.[9]

None of this is very satisfactory, and it is now in serious crisis because of lack of evidence. The scholars who assumed that the title was a current apocalyptic title of honour used to confidently point to Enoch and 4 Esdras as evidence. The Qumran material has brought this view into question, as the caves have produced fragments from every chapter of the Book of Enoch, except chs 37-71. Inter-

---

6. H. E. Todt, *The Son of Man in the Synoptic Tradition* (London, SCM Press, 1965).

7. E. Schweizer, 'The Son of Man', *Journal of Biblical Literature* 79 (1960), pp. 119-129; and *Jesus* (London, SCM Press, 1971), pp. 18-22.

8. P. Vielhauer, Aufsätze zum Neuen Testament (Munchen, Kaiser Verlag, 1965), pp. 50-140; N. Perrin, *Rediscovering the Teaching of Jesus* (London, SCM Press, 1967), pp. 166-194.

9. G. Vermes, *Jesus the Jew* (London, Collins, 1973), pp. 160-191.

estingly enough, this is a section of the book which has always been recognised as 'apart' from the rest of the work. It is a series of parables or 'Similitudes', and it is only here that the title 'the Son of Man' is found. None of this section seems to have been known by the sectarians, and this has caused J. T. Milik and others to argue that the Son of Man section of the Book of Enoch is a later Christian interpolation, and not evidence for a pre-Christian apocalyptic use of the title which may have been formative in the Gospel traditions.[10]

It seems clear from the above confusion that it is time to look at our sources once more. C. F. D. Moule and M. D. Hooker have done this by presenting an interpretation of Dan 7.13, which, they argue, stands behind Jesus' use of the title, and its use in the Synoptic tradition.[11] The figure of the Son of Man in the famous vision represents or symbolises the faithful Israelites during the persecutions of Antiochus IV. What is promised in the vision is that these faithful ones will be finally vindicated. Through obedience to the will of God and humble acceptance of the suffering which this obedience must bring with it, 'the Son of Man' (the faithful Israelites) will be ultimately vindicated in the court of heaven. The certainty of his final vindication gives the Son of Man his authority — he is the one who will have the last word. From this understanding of Dan 7, one can see the Son of Man sayings in the Synoptic Gospels as Jesus' very possible application of this idea to himself, as he has fulfilled the pattern of humble obedience and suffering. However, he is confident in the hope of a final vindication. Its nature could not have been known to Jesus, but we believe that it took place in his resurrection-exaltation. It

10. See especially J. T. Milik, *The Books of Enoch. Aramaic Fragments of Qumran Cave 4* (Oxford, Clarendon Press, 1976). With the collaboration of Matthew Black.

11. C. F. D. Moule, *The Phenomenon of the New Testament*, Studies in Biblical Theology, Second Series 1 (London, SCM Press, 1967), pp. 82-99; M. D. Hooker, *The Son of Man in Mark* (London, SPCK, 1967).

is, then, in the acceptance or refusal of the authority or a refusal to share in the same suffering that men can either gain or lose their own ultimate vindication.

Despite the fact that it has now been proven, especially by the work of C. H. Dodd,[12] that the Johannine Gospel rests upon ancient traditions, related to pre-Synoptic traditions, but which developed along their own trajectory, very few look to the last Gospel's use of the title 'the Son of Man' to see if it can shed light upon the early Church's use of the title. This reticence is explained by the presumption of most scholars that by the time the Fourth Gospel was written (about 100 A.D.) the Son of Man title had lost all its original sense, and was to be identified with the major Johannine titles for Jesus — the Logos and the Son of God. It seems to us, however, that this presumption is not justified by the evidence of the Son of Man sayings in the Gospel. Even a rapid survey of these sayings shows that there is a Johannine Son of Man Christology which adds to our understanding of both the use of the title in the early Church and the Johannine presentation of the person and significance of Jesus.[13]

The first remark that must be made concerns the location of the Johannine Son of Man sayings. A. J. B. Higgins has claimed that the use of the title is 'scattered haphazardly' throughout the first thirteen chapters of the Gospel.[14] It must be noticed that Jn 1-12 deals with the public manifestation of Jesus, and then in 13.31 Jesus announces, in the final Son of Man saying: 'Now has the Son of Man been glorified.' Jesus appears in public at the

---

12. C. H. Dodd, *Historical Tradition in the Fourth Gospel* (Cambridge, University Press, 1965).

13. I have attempted to prove this point in two works: *The Johannine Son of Man*, Biblioteca de Scienze Religiose 14 (Rome, LAS, 1978[2]); 'The Johannine Son of Man', *Biblical Theology Bulletin* 6 (1976), pp. 177-189. What follows is a simplification of this article.

14. A. J. B. Higgins, *Jesus and the Son of Man* (London, Lutterworth, 1964), p. 155.

end of the book, in his Passion. Again, something allied to the title appears as Pilate points to Jesus and announces: 'Behold the man!' It appears that limitation of the title 'the Son of Man' to the *public* appearances of Jesus may be an important indication that its use has something to say about the *public* manifestation of God in and through Jesus. A survey of the sayings themselves confirms this indication.

2. *The Sayings*

John 1.51

Because of the awkward change from singular to plural in 'And he said to *him*, "Truly, truly I say to *you* (plural), you (plural) will see the heaven opened and the angels of God ascending and descending upon the Son of Man" ' (Jn 1.51), many scholars regard this strange saying as a detached saying about the Son of Man, added to the otherwise homogeneous passage of 1.43-50. Whatever the pre-history of this passage may have been, importance must be given to the uniquely Johannine use of the double 'amen'.[15] The Evangelist shows, by his use of this solemn introduction, that he wishes to make a point which he considered important. He may have taken the saying from somewhere else, but we can only speculate about that. The question which must be asked is: what does this saying mean in its present context?

The verse comes at the end of a long series of titles, given to Jesus by the Evangelist or other people (vv. 20, 21a, 21b, 29, 34, 41, 45, 49). Jesus' reply to the acclamations of others is found in v. 51, and he replies in terms of 'greater things' which his disciples will *see* in the ascending and descending of angels upon the Son of Man. Here John could be using a traditional pattern, according to which Jesus replied to other titles in terms of the Son of Man (see Mk 8.31 parrs; Mk 14.61-62 parrs). In Jn 1.19-49

15. The double 'amen' is found *only* in John in the New Testament. It appears 24 times.

the belief of the early Church is certainly reflected, but John indicates another point of view. Using a current understanding of the scene of Jacob's dream from Gen 28.12, John speaks of Jesus as the place where God communicates with man. There is no historical fulfillment of the scene, as the disciples are promised that they 'will see' the revelation of God in the Son of Man. The use of the verb 'to see' in the Fourth Gospel frequently refers to faith in the revelation of God, which can be 'seen' or 'not seen', according to the response of the one called to faith in Jesus. This is most clearly shown in Jn 9, but is frequent in the whole Gospel (see 3.36; 11.4a; 16.16; Jn 3.2). The disciples will be called to believe in this revelation. Jn 1.51 must be understood as programmatic for the whole of the public revelation of God in the appearance of the Johannine Jesus; it is the promise of the Son of Man.

John 3.13-15

As we have already seen, Jn 3 has a puzzling mixture of narrative, monologue and reflection which has always caused difficulty for the interpreter. We have argued that 2.23-3.36 must be seen as a section of the passage from Cana to Cana (2.1 — 4.54) which deals with the problem of various types of faith. In our passage Nicodemus shows incomplete faith (3.1-10) and is corrected in a reflection from Jesus (vv. 11-21) while the Baptist shows correct faith (vv. 22-30), and this leads to a reflection from the Evangelist (vv. 31-36).[16]

Within this context we again find 'the Son of Man' used by Jesus to correct an incomplete confession of faith (see v. 2). Vv. 13-15 must be understood as a statement about Jesus as the revealer of the heavenly things mentioned in v. 12. Jesus' words are directed against the suggestions of a current stream of Jewish piety, which claimed that the great saints of Israel (Moses, Elijah, Isaiah etc.) had ascended to receive their knowledge of God, and then

---

16. See above, pp. 57-59.

descended to reveal it. Jesus does not say that *he* ascended, but that *no-one (oudeis)* has ascended to see God and find out about him so that he could descend again to reveal him. There is only one who can reveal God with ultimate authority — the Son of Man, who has descended in the incarnation to reveal God to men.[17] As this is the case, then vv. 14-15 can be readily understood as the further specification of what has been said in v. 13. As Jesus *is* the unique revealer of God, John can now tell us how that revelation takes place (v. 14), and spell out its consequences (v. 15). The Son of Man who is the unique revealer must be lifted up on a cross, so that all may look upon him and have eternal life in him (see Num 21.8-9). If the unique importance of the Son of Man had not been clearly stated in v. 13, then there would be no point in vv. 14-15. The parallel drawn with the serpent on a stake must be kept; it refers to the paradox of the Johannine Cross, which is at once a 'lifting up' of Jesus on a cross and his exaltation and enthronement.[18]

In vv. 13-15 we meet, for the first time, the indication that the Son of Man title is intimately linked with the human Jesus. It is used to speak of Jesus who has 'descended' in the incarnation, and who was lifted up on a cross. The event of the crucifixion is an eminently human event. Only a man can be nailed to a cross, and the lifting up of Jesus on the Cross is always spoken of in terms of 'the Son of Man' (see 8.28; 12.23,34). Never do we hear of the crucifixion of the Son of God!

---

17. Many English translations (New English Bible, Jerusalem Bible, Knox Bible) have 'who is in heaven' in v. 13. This is not found in the best manuscripts, and should be omitted (as in the Revised Standard Version).

18. This double sense is given by the use of the verb *hupsothenai*, which can mean both 'to lift up' in a physical sense, and 'to exalt' in the sense of a raising in honour. See W. Thüsing, *Die Erhöhung und Verherrlichung Jesu im Johannesevangelium*, Neutestamentliche Abhandlungen 21/1 (Munster, Aschendorff, 1970[2]), pp. 3-37.

Our next saying appears in ch. 5. which, as we have already
seen,[19] is greatly concerned with the Johannine understanding of Jesus as the Son of God. Throughout the first
part of the discourse (vv. 19-30) Jesus speaks of his relationship to his Father, and the consequences of that
relationship. In v. 22 we are told that all judgment has been
given to the Son by the Father. However, when Jesus
speaks of the *exercising* of judgment, he speaks of himself
as 'the Son of Man' (v. 27). The verses which follow (vv.
28-29) speak of some sort of future judgment. John usually
speaks of judgment as already taking place (see v. 25), but
the Fourth Gospel's idea of 'realised' eschatology is carefully balanced by a word about the other side of death, and
the traditional future eschatology is found, for example, in
5.28-29. Jn 5.27 is dependent upon the Greek translation
of Dan 7.13-14 — also the background for the Synoptic
Son of Man sayings — and could well be the oldest application of the title, taken directly from Dan 7.13, to Jesus.
As in the Greek vision of Dan 7.13, the title is used here
without an article ('a Son of Man') and may refer to the
'humanness' of Jesus, but it must also be understood as a
title, and as the specification of Jesus' role as judge. He is
able to exercise judgment, *because* he is Son of Man. In vv.
24-25 reference is made to the self-judgment of men
through their reaction to the revelation brought by and in
Jesus. This is continued into v. 27. The Johannine Son of
Man is 'where judgment takes place' in the way described in
vv. 24-25. The theme of judgment was very important in
the Synoptic Gospels' presentation of Jesus as the Son of
Man (see, for example, Mk 8.38; 13.26; Matt 13.41; 16.13;
26.2; Lk 6.22; 7.34; 9.58; 17.24-26; 22.48 etc.), and again
John's link with the older traditions can be felt. In 3.15 we
learnt that anyone who believes in the elevated Son of Man
has eternal life. It is implicit, therefore, that those who
refuse to believe shall die. This is the judgment that the

---

19. See above, pp. 59-62.

Johannine Son of Man exercises.

John 6.27,53,62

The sixth chapter of the Fourth Gospel is one of the most moving pieces of literature in the New Testament. With great artistry John has unfolded his teaching in the following fashion:

(I)   6.1-4:   Introduction to the theme and to the Players

                Where : Sea of Galilee —
                            Mountain (vv. 1 and 3)
                When : Passover (v. 4)
                Why : Signs (v. 2)
                Who : A multitude and the disciples
                            (vv. 2 and 3)

(II) 6.5-21: Two miracle stories

                (i) vv. 5-15 : The miracle of the Loaves and Fishes and the raising of false messianic hopes (vv. 14-15).

                (ii) vv. 16-21: The correction of that hope—at least among his disciples — in the revelation of Jesus as 'I am' (v. 20).

(III) 6.22-24: Transition scene. The players are again introduced and a further development of the theme is indicated.

                Where : Capernaum (v. 24)
                When : Next day (closer to Passover) (vv. 22)
                Why : Seek Jesus (they had not been present at the revelation of Jesus as 'I am') (v. 24).
                Who : The people who had eaten the bread (v. 23).

(IV) 6.25-59: The discourse on the bread from heaven which (who) gives eternal life.

(V) 6.60-71: Two possible reactions to the revelation

80

of Jesus as the Bread of Life.

    (i) vv. 60-65 : The reaction of 'many of his disciples' who leave Jesus.

    (ii) vv. 66-71 : The confession of Peter, who accepts Jesus.

Within this dense presentation of the person and significance of Jesus, 'the true bread from heaven', he is thrice called 'the Son of Man' (vv. 27,53,62).

In 6.27 Jesus is again correcting the false messianic hopes expressed by vv. 14-15. He has already revealed himself to his disciples as 'I am' on the lake (vv. 16-21), but the crowd which assembles in vv. 22-24 still seek him for the wrong reasons. He corrects their false hopes in terms of 'the Son of Man'. Their hopes for a second Moses and eschatological manna are vain.[20] He offers, instead, a revelation which will endure and which will produce eternal life, and he offers it to men in his role as the Son of Man.

The reference to the Son of Man in 6.53 certainly contains eucharistic overtones, but the message of the revelation of the Son of Man and the life to be found therein, so dominant in vv. 27-47, is still present. As in other eucharistic passages in the New Testament (Mk 14.22-26; Matt 26.26-30; Lk 22.15-20, I Cor 11.23-25), the Cross is also central to John's thought here, introduced by v. 51c: 'The bread which I shall give is my flesh for the life of the world.' John continues to develop his Christology of the

---

20. The Jews' expectations of vv. 14-15 reflect their conviction that the Messiah would be announced by a second Moses and another miracle of manna. See, for example, the sentiments of a book written in the second half of the first century: 'And it shall come to pass at that self-same time that the treasury of manna shall again descend from on high, and they will eat of it in those years, because these are those who have come to the consummation of time. And it shall come to pass after these things, when the time of the advent of the Messiah is fulfilled, that he shall return in glory' (2 Baruch 29.8-30.1).

Son of Man as the place, among men, where God is revealed. The food which remains forever (v. 27) is to be had in the full acceptance, in faith, of the revelation of God by and in the Son of Man, which will reach its climax on Calvary (v. 53). This is not mere mysticism, however, as it can be experienced in the celebration of the Eucharist.[21]

Jesus' reply to the dissatisfaction of his listeners in the difficult vv. 62-63 is not to be regarded as a reference to an ascension which will either condemn or save them. Jesus does not want to discourage them further, so he asks a rhetorical question: 'And if you were to see the Son of Man ascend?' There is no need for this, as Jesus adds 'to where he was before'! Because of his pre-existence as the Logos, the Word made flesh in the Son of Man is the fulness of God's revelation. Recalling 3.13 and the Jewish speculations which stood behind that saying,[22] Jesus reminds his listeners that he has no need to ascend because he comes from above. He was there 'before' and thus the authoritative words which he has spoken to them are spirit and life (v. 63).

John 8.28

As Jesus moves closer to the end of his ministry, the conflict with his opponents becomes more marked, In Jn 8.12-30 we have a last effort on the part of Jesus to give witness to the light (v. 12) before an unbelieving audience. We see the first part of the discourse in ch. 8 as running from vv. 12-30, and as positive in tone. It is not 'too late' for the Jews, and their questions (see especially the difficult v. 25) are not hostile but rather ignorant. That this is the case is indicated by the conclusion of the section:

---

21. See my further considerations, 'John 6 and the Celebration of the Eucharist', *The Downside Review* 93 (1975), pp. 243-251.

22. See above, pp. 77-78.

'many believed in him' *(episteusan eis auton)* (v. 30).[23]
The second section concludes ominously: 'so they took up
stones to throw at him' (v. 59).

In the more positive section of the discourse Jesus
reveals himself as the one 'from above', and he speaks of
himself as 'I am he'. They must believe in this unique revelation brought by Jesus if they are to be saved (vv. 23-24).
This announcement meets with a total lack of understanding (v. 25a) and draws an exclamation of frustration
from Jesus in 'a mood of yearning impatience.'[24] Despite
the obtuseness of his audience, Jesus shows a continual
resolve to do the will of his Father (v. 26). That this
interpretation is correct is confirmed by the editorial note
of v. 27: 'They did not understand that he was speaking to
them of the Father.' In a final attempt to convince them,
he announces that his true identity will be recognised when
they have lifted up the Son of Man: 'When you have lifted
up the Son of Man, then you will know that I am he.'
Throughout the passage Jesus has been concerned with his
origin 'from above' and his being sent by the Father (vv.
14, 16, 18, 19, 21, 23, 26, 27, 28, 29). Because this is true
he is the one who can authentically reveal the Father.
Unless the Jews believe this they will die in their sins (v.
24). Despite their obtuseness (vv. 25-27), they will be able
to look upon the Son of Man whom they have lifted up on
a cross, and there they will find God's revelation to men (v.
28). This is the significance of the identification of Jesus
with the 'I am he' formula. By using this formula John

---

23. In v. 30 the verb *pisteuein* is used with *eis*, while in v.
31 the same verb is followed by a dative. This could be an
indication of two different types of faith. The second type (v.
31) is insufficient. See R. E. Brown, *John*, pp. 513-515 and
the bibliography mentioned there. Against this distinction is
R. Bultmann, Art. *'pisteuo'*, *TDNT* VI, pp. 222-223.

24. R. H. Strachan, *The Fourth Gospel, Its Significance
and Environment* (London, SCM Press, 1941[3]), p. 209. This is
a difficult verse. For a summary of other possible translations,
see R. E. Brown, *John*, pp. 347-348.

identifies Jesus with the God who revealed himself in this way in the Old Testament, especially in the Pentateuch (see Exod 14.4,18; 20.2,5; 29.46; Lev 19 passim; 20.17) and in Second Isaiah (see such passages as 43.10 and 45.18). Jn 8.28, therefore, claims that the elevated Son of Man will always be the place where man can find God's revelation to men and judge himself by accepting or refusing it.

John 9.35

The importance of 'the Son of Man' for Johannine Christology is made clear in 9.35, where the man born blind is asked, after a gradual progression towards the light (see vv. 11, 17, 35), to confess his faith in the Son of Man. Nowhere else in the New Testament is the Son of Man made the object of a profession of faith. When the man enquires who this Son of Man is, Jesus replies: 'You have seen him and it is he who speaks to you' (v. 37). The Son of Man is thus identified with the revealer — the one who is 'seen' and the one who 'speaks'. Against this progression towards the true light of the authentic revelation of God, John sets the failure of the Pharisees to see and understand this light which Jesus, the Son of Man, brings. He is the revelation of God among men, the light of the world (v. 5), the manifestation of God to men (v. 3) who can be seen and heard (v. 37) by people who are prepared to see and hear him (v. 39). In their decision they judge themselves according to their choice of the light or the darkness (vv. 39-41). Again Jesus is presented as the unique revealer of God, and consequently as the place of judgment. It is not necessary to find other New Testament passages where the Son of Man is made the object of a confession of faith. It is sufficient to recognise what this title meant in the Johannine Church: Jesus as the place where God's revelation is to be found and, consequently, as the place where men will judge themselves. As this is the case, it is not at all strange to find the Johannine Jesus asking: 'Do you believe in the Son of Man?'

John 12,23.34

Introduced by the prophetic announcement of Caiphas
(11.45-53) and the arrival of the final Passover feast (11.55;
12.1), Jn 12 is dominated by the coming passion. The hints
given throughout the Gospel that the supreme moment of
the revelation of the Son of Man would take place on the
Cross (1.13-14; 6.27,53; 8.28) are now made fully explicit
in 12,23.34. In the context of an anointing for death and a
prophecy of the betrayal, his entry into Jerusalem is
presented as the acclamation of a political messiah by
John's reference to the palm fronds, and his addition of
'the King of Israel' to the quotation from Ps. 118 (v. 13).[25]
On hearing of the advent of the representatives of the
Gentile world Jesus can now proclaim, against the false
messianic hopes aroused by his entry, that 'the hour has
come for the Son of Man to be glorified' (v. 23). The
glorification referred to in this context must be the Cross,
and this is made clearer in vv. 32-33. The Jews, however,
will not accept this Son of Man, as they have their own
ideas about the Messiah (v. 34). They have failed to
understand the Johannine Son of Man and 'walk in the
darkness' (v. 35).

John 13.31

After the conclusion of the public ministry the passion
starts with the symbolic washing of the feet and Judas'
betrayal of Jesus. Jesus announces the arrival of the passion
by saying: 'Now is the Son of Man glorified and in him God
is glorified' (13.31). Jn. 13.31-32 is closely linked with
17.1-5. There seem to be two moments in the glorification
of Jesus. Firstly Jesus is glorified and glorifies God on the
Cross (13.31), with the perfection of the task 'on earth'
which the Father had entrusted to Jesus (17.4. See also
19.28-30). Secondly, intimately linked with the same
'hour', is the glory which will come to the Son when he

---

25. See W. R. Farmer, 'The Palm Branches in John 12.13',
Journal of Theological Studies 3 (1952), pp. 62-66.

returns to that glory which was his with the Father 'before the world was made' (17.5; 13.32. See 1.1-2;14). It is only in the context of the *human* manifestation of the glory of God in Jesus that John uses the title 'the Son of Man'. The human Jesus, especially in his being lifted up on the Cross, is the place, on earth, where men can see the revelation of God. Once Jesus, *through* the hour of the Cross, returns to his Father, to where he was 'before the world was made' (see 1.1-2 and 17.5), he is never referred to as 'the Son of Man', but as 'the Son' (17.1.5).

John 19.5

All the Son of Man sayings point, ultimately, to the Cross. In the trial scene before Pilate the significance of the Johannine Cross is fully explained. At the centre of this scene, Jesus is ironically crowned (19.1-3), after which he comes before the crowd, still dressed as a king, and Pilate proclaims: 'Here he is — the Man' (19.5). This is probably the final indication that the promises initiated in 1.51 are now fulfilled.

3. *Conclusions*

Some conclusions can be drawn from this rapid survey. John presents Jesus as the Son of Man when he wants to point to the incarnation of God's revelation, bringing judgment in its presence in history. Why has John used the title 'the Son of Man' to convey this message? There is no need to look beyond the traditional Son of Man figure for an answer to that question, although one must allow that John has refurbished traditional themes in almost every instance. This comes about from a profoundly different vision of Jesus. Hooker and Moule have suggested that the Son of Man is a figure whose humble obedience and consequent suffering will be vindicated in his resurrection. In John the glorification and vindication of the Son of Man takes place on the Cross. This is so because Jesus comes from God. What was traditionally 'outside' time can now be comfortably drawn back into John's enigmatic theology of a glorification on the Cross. Given this change of viewpoint, the contacts between the two traditions are very strong:

(a) In Jn 5.27 we have a direct link with Dan 7.13. The Synoptic tradition uses Dan 7 for the apocalyptic appearance of Jesus at the end of history. John draws this judgment back into history, in line with his theology of 'realised eschatology'.

(b) Almost every Johannine Son of Man saying comes as a concluding statement on the lips of Jesus, resolving a series of questions or insufficient confessions about the person of Jesus (1.51; 3.13-14; 6.27; 8.28; 9.35; 12.23,34). This repeats a traditional pattern in the Synoptic Gospels, where Jesus replied to his interlocutors — who had suggested their own answers concerning his person and role — in terms of 'the Son of Man' (Mk 8.27-9,1; Matt 16.13-28; Lk 9.18-27; Mk 14.61-62; Matt 26.63-64; Lk 22.67-71).

(c) Twice in the Fourth Gospel we are told that the Son of Man *must (dei)* be lifted up (3.14; 12.34) and once it is announced that the Jews will lift up the Son of Man (8.28). There is a close link here with the threefold passion prediction of the Synoptic tradition (Mk 8.31; 9.31; 10.33-34 parrs). For the Synoptics this is Jesus' lowest moment — but for John he is 'lifted up' to his glorification.

(d) The Johannine Son of Man refers to the historical presence of Jesus, the revelation of God among men — a revelation which reaches its high point on the Cross. The Synoptic Son of Man is also present among men, and a suffering figure, but he is a future judge. This future Son of Man, so central to the Synoptic tradition, has been drawn back into history by John, as man is judged by his acceptance or refusal of the revelation brought by and in the Son of Man.

Throughout, we are dealing with the Johannisation of a traditional theme.

It is a serious misunderstanding of the Johannine Jesus to identify the significance of 'the Son of Man' with that of 'the Logos' or 'the Son of God'. John uses his language carefully, and he has a specific theological point to make when he presents Jesus as 'the Son of God'. As we have already seen, Jesus' union of love with the Father is rooted in a relationship which exists outside time and space. It begins in the Father (1.14) and ends in the Father (17.5); it is pre-existent, incarnate and resumed in the glorification of the Son *through* the Cross. Not so the Son of Man. The title is strictly limited to the human, historical appearance of Jesus of Nazareth. The Son of Man is glorified in the very human experience *on* the Cross. There is no crucifixion of the Son of God, but neither is there a pre-existent Son of Man.

John has taken the term 'the Son of Man' from Christian tradition. He has used the term in a way which betrays his own theological stance in every instance, but the Johannine Son of Man is the continuation of a dynamic, growing interpretation of Dan 7.13 which can be found in the Synoptic Gospel, Enoch, 4 Esdras,[26] the Fourth Gospel, and which even extends into the writings of the early Fathers. Between the earlier use of the Son of Man who would come at the end of time as judge, and the Fathers' use of the term to speak of Jesus' human condition (see especially Ignatius, *Eph.* 20.2; Barnabas, 12.10; and Hippolytus, *Contra Noetum*, 2.15) there is certainly a change of interest. Perhaps John's use of the term provides the link. His contact with the traditional Son of Man on the one hand, and his accentuation of the human figure on the other, could well place him at the cross-roads between the New Testament and the Fathers of the early Church.

---

26. We include Enoch and 4 Esdras, while maintaining that they were not elements in the formation of the Gospel traditions. There is what C. F. D. Moule, *The Phenomenon of the New Testament*, p. 83, calls 'a common fund of thoughts behind them'.

Irenaeus certainly sounds very Johannine when he writes of the Son of Man:

> The Word of God which lived among men became the Son of Man, so that man might look upon God, and that God might dwell among men
>
> (*Adv. Haer.* III.21.2).

Chapter 5

THE MESSIAH

The most outstanding testimony to the Jewish roots of Christianity is found in its very name, coming from the word 'Christ'. Our faith is rooted in Jesus Christ. As Paul tells the Romans: 'Those who receive the abundance of grace and the free gift of righteousness reign in life through the one man Jesus Christ' (Rom 5.17). The name 'Christ' belongs to Jesus because the early Church believed that he was the Messiah, the fulfillment of the hopes of Israel. As the early Church spoke Greek, so the Hebrew/Aramaic term 'Messiah' (the anointed one) was translated into Greek *ho christos* (from the Greek verb *chrio*: to anoint). The man called 'Jesus' is now seen as 'Jesus the Christ' or simply, Jesus Christ. In fact, we generally speak of him today as Christ, and we call ourselves Christians.

All of the Gospels speak of Jesus as the Christ (Mark 8 times; Matthew 17 times; Luke 13 times) and John is no exception. He uses the term more than the other Evangelists (21 times), and this has led J. A. T. Robinson to argue that 'This, rather than "the Logos", is the category which controls his Christology in the body of the Gospel.'[1] Bishop Robinson is convinced that the Gospel was a product of Judaea, and that it was directed to Greek-speaking Jews. John's purpose was to prove to them that Jesus of Nazareth was the Christ (see 20.31). Another scholar who argues a similar case is W. C. van Unnik. He claims that scholarship does an injustice to the reference to Jesus as 'the Christ' in 20.31, always running on to see this passage, indicating the reason why John wrote his Gospel, as a call to faith in Jesus as the Son of God. Van

---

1. J. A. T. Robinson, 'The Destination and Purpose of St. John's Gospel', *New Testament Studies* 6 (1959-60), p. 122. The article runs from pp. 117-131. In his recent book, *Redating the New Testament* Robinson does not make so much of the Messiah question, but the argument of this earlier article stands behind his conclusions on pp. 292-293.

Unnik also thinks that the Gospel was written for the conversion of diaspora Jews to a faith in Jesus as "the Messiah".[2]

In our previous chapters we have seen the central role played by such titles as 'the Logos', 'the Son of God' and 'the Son of Man'. Can the same be said for 'the Christ'? The number of times that the title appears is an indication that it says something for the Evangelist, and van Unnik is partly correct when he writes: 'In the synagogue there was a law-suit with the issue "is Jesus the Messiah or not?" '[3] If, however, our consideration of the *milieu* which gave birth to the Gospel is correct,[4] this law-suit has already reached its verdict: Jesus was *not* the Messiah, and anyone who believed that he was had to leave the synagogue. If this is the case, why does John use the title so frequently?[5]

It is not enough to notice the number of times the title is used; it is more important to see who uses it, and why it is used. Both Robinson and van Unnik are correct in seeing that the use of 'the Christ' points to Judaism, but the Johannine Gospel was not written to *convert* Greek-speaking Jews. C. H. Dodd has stated the relationship between John and Judaism succinctly when he wrote: 'Nowhere else in the New Testament do we find Christian belief in the Christ *so clearly at issue* with the Jewish beliefs out of which in the last resort it

---

2. W. C. van Unnik, 'The Purpose of St. John's Gospel', in *The Gospels Reconsidered: A Selection of Papers read at the International Congress on the Four Gospels in 1957* (Oxford, Blackwell, 1960), pp. 167-196.

3. *ibid.*, p. 185.

4. See above, pp. 20-23.

5. The answer which we give to this question is not new. It is spelt out in greater detail by R. Schnackenburg, 'Die Messiasfrage im Johannesevangelium', in J. Blinzler — O. Kuss — F. Mussner (eds.), *Neutestamentliche Aufsätze: Festschrift J. Schmid zum 70. Geburtstag* (Regensburg, Pustet, 1963), pp. 240-264; and M. de Jonge, 'Jewish Expectations about the "Messiah" according to the Fourth Gospel', *New Testament Studies*, 19 (1972-73), pp. 246-270.

arose.'[6] In our introductory chapter we argued that John's problem was Jewish, but not one of conversion. We see it, rather, as John's word to his Church as it was forcibly dismissed from its Jewish roots, and thus obliged to discover its true self in the syncretistic world of Asia Minor. The Messiah-problem must have been central in this discussion. The Synagogue refused to believe that Jesus was the Christ, and excluded anyone who claimed that he was. If this was the situation, one could understandably see the Gospel as an aggressive claim that Jesus *was* the Christ, but that would hardly have solved the problems of a Church which now had to establish itself in a non-Jewish world. John saw Jesus as something more than 'the Christ'. E. F. Scott once claimed that John's attitude to this question reflected that of Jesus. This may or may not be true, but of John it could be said that 'He . . . was conscious that the ancient title [Messiah] was not fully adequate, and sought to inform it with a new content.'[7] This can be seen from a survey of John's use of the title which takes notice of who says it, and why they say it.

1. *John the Baptist*

   We have already seen that John the Baptist's role in this Gospel is to be a witness to Jesus.[8] This role was threatened by any attempt to make the Baptist the central figure. Thus, on two occasions he protests: 'I am not the Christ' (1.20; 3.28).

2. *Other actors in the drama, who are guessing at Jesus' role and significance*

   The overwhelming majority of the uses of 'the Christ' fall into this category. The first chapter of the Gospel has to be understood as a series of guesses from various people who react to the presence of Jesus. The use of these titles must be understood in the light of current messianic expecta-

---

6. C. H. Dodd, *Interpretation*, p. 229. Stress mine.

7. E. F. Scott, *The Fourth Gospel. Its Purpose and Theology* (Edinburgh, T. and T. Clark, 1908), p. 183.

8. See above, pp. 44-45.

tions (see vv. 20, 21a, 21b, 29, 34, 41, 45, 49).[9] The Pharisees ask the Baptist about his being the Christ (v. 25) and Andrew tells Simon Peter that he has found the Messiah (v. 41). As we have already pointed out, Jesus does not accept these suggestions from his first followers, who are struggling to identify him. Instead of their guesses he promises the sight of 'greater things' in the Son of Man (vv. 50-51).[10]

On two occasions in ch. 4 the Samaritan woman wonders whether or not Jesus is the Christ (4.25,29). The passage from vv. 25-26 is the closest the Gospel comes to an identification on the part of Jesus with the Messiah. In fact, our English translations make the identification. The Samaritan woman says: 'I know that Messiah is coming (he who is called Christ); when he comes, he will show us all things' (v. 25), and Jesus replies: 'I who speak to you am he' (v. 26). This misrepresents the Greek by separating 'I . . . am he'. A literal translation of the Greek reads: 'I am (is) the one speaking to you.' As in 1.50-51 Jesus takes guesswork one step further by identifying himself, not as the Christ, but as 'I am' *(Ego eimi)*.[11] There is, of course, no denial of Jesus' being the Messiah, but his Messiahship will not be determined by the Messianic expectations of the people who interrogate him. He is the Christ, but in a sense not even imagined by his questioner. The woman shows that she has not fully understood by rushing off to her townsfolk, asking them: 'Can this be the Christ?' (v. 29). She was left wondering at Jesus' telling her of her

9. See R. Schnackenburg, *The Gospel According to St John* (London, Burns and Oates, 1968), Vol. I, pp. 507-514: 'Excursus III: The Titles of Jesus in John 1'.

10. See above, pp. 76-77.

11. Many commentators merely see this as an identification of Jesus with the Samaritan hopes for a Messiah. See, for example, R. E. Brown, *John*, p. 197-173. See, on the other hand, R. Schnackenburg, *St. John*, pp. 441-442; B. Lindars, *John*, p. 191; and E. Hoskyns, *Fourth Gospel*, pp. 244-245.

disastrous marital situation, but the townsfolk come to true faith — not through some messianic expectation which they could determine — they 'believed because of his word' (v. 41; see also v. 42).[12]

Jn 7-8 is highlighted by Jesus' encounter with 'the Jews' at the Feast of Tabernacles. Central to this encounter is the Jews' attempt to understand Jesus as Christ. The crux of their failure to understand Jesus can be found in the following passages:

> 7.26-27: 'Some of the people of Jerusalem therefore said, "Is not this the man whom they seek to kill? And here he is, speaking openly, and they say nothing to him! Can it be that the authorities really know that this is the Christ? Yet *we know where this man comes from*; and when the Christ appears, no one will know where he comes from." '

> 7.40-43: 'Some of the people said, "This is really the prophet." Others said *"Is the Christ to come from Galilee?* Has not the scripture said that *the Christ is descended from David, and comes from Bethlehem*, the village where David was?" So there was a division among the people over him.'

We claimed that the people who speak of Jesus as the Christ are generally 'guessing'. This is especially clear here. The people are desperately trying to fit Jesus into their own categories — categories of Jewish Messianic expectations which *they* could use as a yardstick to measure Jesus! Is he 'the Prophet'? Does he come from David's city? We should not know his origin? In fact, they are wrong with all their guessing. The Church that John wrote for knew that he was not the Prophet who was going to usher in the end time, according to Jewish hopes (see Deut 18.18). They

---

12. See above, pp. 23-24, where our division of the Gospel shows the progression in faith (no faith — incomplete faith — complete faith) which is central to an understanding of the passage 'from Cana to Cana' (2.1 — 4.54).

also knew that he *did* come from Bethlehem.[13] The crux of the matter, however, lies in the conviction of the Jews that they knew 'where this man comes from' (vv. 27,42). Thinking that they can determine his place of origin as Galilee (which is, in itself, wrong!), they have failed to understand the significance of Jesus and his claims. It is vital that they understand and believe that he is 'from above' and 'from God'. Only when they are prepared to make this step will they be able to accept Jesus' revelation of the Father whom he reveals authentically, precisely because he is 'from God'. Their Messianic hopes do not take them to this point — and thus they are inadequate.

Now we can understand the incompleteness of the faith of some of the people who believed, saying: 'When the Christ appears, will he do more signs than this man has done?' (7.31). The signs which would accompany the arrival of the Messiah are not enough for a correct understanding of the Johannine Jesus — they must lead the believer to see and understand 'where this man comes from' (v. 27).[14] This same arrogant refusal of Jesus because he does not fulfill Jewish Messianic hopes is seen in 12.34: 'We have heard from the law that Christ remains forever. How can you say that the Son of Man must be lifted up?' Here the conflict between the *Johannine* idea of the person and role of Jesus, who must go to the Cross to reveal God to men, and the Jewish idea of 'the Christ', who will remain forever,[15] is especially clear. Jesus is something different — something much more — than the Jewish Messiah. The inability of 'the Jews' to see that it is Jesus' union with his

13. Some scholars point to Jn 7.42 to show that John knew nothing of the Matthean and Lucan birth narratives (see Matt 2.1,5-8,16; Lk 2.4.15). See, for example, R. Bultmann, *John*, p. 306, note 6: 'The Evangelist knows nothing, or wants to know nothing of the birth in Bethlehem.' In fact, given the irony of the passage, the contrary is the case! See R. E. Brown, *John*, pp. 329-330.

14. See M. de Jonge, 'Jewish Expectations about the "Messiah" ', pp. 257-262.

Father, i.e., his Sonship, that most fully explains his person and mission is seen again in 10.24. As usual, they demand that Jesus speak to them of himself in categories which they can understand: 'If you are the Christ, tell us plainly.' He refuses to do so, insisting that he can only be understood in terms of his relationship with God, whom he calls his Father (vv. 25-30), concluding with his stunning claim: 'I and the Father are one' (v. 30). Little wonder that the Jews, locked in their own preconceived ideas of who Jesus must be, answer this claim by 'taking up stones to stone him' (v. 31).

The one remaining confession of Jesus as the Christ comes from Martha, who chastises Jesus for not coming when Lazarus was ill (11.21). In 11.25-26 Jesus replies to her by explaining that he is the resurrection and the life. Looking back to 5.19-30, Jesus explains that he, like his Father, can give life to those who believe in him. When Martha is asked if she believes all this she replies: 'Yes, Lord; I believe that you are the Christ, the Son of God, he who is coming into the world' (11.27). This is normally taken as a correct confession of Jesus, but does the context allow this interpretation? We have argued above that Martha's confession of Jesus as 'the Son of God' and 'the one who is to come' must be understood as the expression of Jewish Messianic hopes.[16] The same must be said of her understanding of Jesus as 'the Christ'. This is clearly indicated by the very next verse, where she calls Jesus 'the teacher' (v. 28), and the general atmosphere of disbelief in vv. 28-40, made especially evident in Martha's words of v. 39. If she had truly understood what Jesus had said in vv. 25-26, a fact which is presupposed if we are to give the confession of v. 27 its full Johannine significance, then how

---

15. It is not clear what part of 'the law' makes this statement about the Messiah. It is most probably Ps 88.37. See W. C. van Unnik, 'The Quotation from the Old Testament in John 12,34', *Novum Testamentum* 3 (1959), pp. 174-179.

16. See above, pp. 64-65.

could she possibly reply to Jesus' command, 'Take away the stone', with the words of v. 39: 'Lord, by this time there will be an odour, for he has been dead four days'? Martha, like *all* the others who wonder about Jesus' person and role, has not seen through to the basis of Jesus' life and action. Jesus himself explains it in vv. 41b-42 through a prayer which he prays 'that they may believe that thou dost send me' (v. 42). Jesus' interlocutors *never* seem to be able to make this leap out of time, space and the limitations of their own Jewishness to see that Jesus cannot be understood apart from his relationship with the Father, who sent him.

3. *The Evangelist*

In a search for the message of any of the Gospels the most important indications are always found in those passages where the Evangelist himself is speaking. Words of Jesus and the questions, answers and reactions of the other players in the drama often come to John from his sources, but when he writes a prologue and conclusion to his own Gospel, or when he interrupts the narrative with his own comments, then they must be understood as 'stage directions' in which the mind of the author is most clearly manifested.

From the evidence which we have surveyed so far, it has become clear that Jesus can be misunderstood if he is seen only as 'the Christ'. The Jews are asked to go further, to look to his origin, to 'where he comes from', to find that he is what he is because of his relationship with God, his Father, who sent him. John's own comments make this even clearer.

In the Prologue to the Gospel, the name of Jesus appears only once, in v. 17. There we are told: 'For the law was given through Moses; the gift of the truth came through Jesus Christ.' There is no need for us to repeat here what we have already said about these two 'gifts',[17] but the word 'Christ' here has become a part of Jesus' proper name.

17. See above, pp. 50-52.

Nevertheless, there is an indication here that Jesus is, for John, in some way 'the Christ'. In 9.22, as we have already shown, the situation of the Johannine Church is clearly shown: 'His parents said this because they feared the Jews, for the Jews had already agreed that if anyone should confess him to be Christ, he was to be put out of the Synagogue.'[18] These two passages show us that there must be a sense in which the Johannine Church did believe in Jesus as the Christ. This sense is indicated in the remaining two comments from the Evangelist.

17.3, although found in the apostolic prayer of Jesus, is universally admitted as a clarifying note added by the Evangelist.[19] Here John again gives Jesus the proper name of 'Jesus Christ'. Jesus is the Christ, but only in so far as he is the revealer of the only God, who sent him into the world that we may have life: 'And this is eternal life, that they know thee the only true God, and Jesus Christ whom thou hast sent' (17.3). This is poles apart from the Christ that the Jews wanted to find in him. The final use of 'the Christ' is found in 20.31, where the theme of 17.3 is repeated: 'These things are written that you may believe that Jesus is the Christ, the Son of God, and that believing you may have life in his name.' What John has been hinting at throughout the whole of the Gospel is now made clear. Jesus *is* the Christ, but not the Christ of Jewish expectations; he is the Christ only in so far as he is the Son of God.

4. *Conclusion*

Bishop Robinson saw the two terms of 20.31 as explaining one another, but claimed that Jesus' Sonship was to be

---

18. See above, pp. 20-22.

19. We cannot argue this at length. If one reads 17.1-5, omitting v. 3, it is immediately apparent that v. 3 is an explanatory addition. What must be insisted upon is that precisely because v. 3 is John's explanation of what he is trying to say, it takes on, rather than loses, significance.

understood in terms of his being the Messiah.[20] The evidence seems to point in the other direction. John is writing into a situation where old categories have to be given new meanings. As we have already seen, the Johannine Jesus can only be understood if we are prepared to grant that he pre-existed as 'the Logos' and that he is, before time, during his earthly existence, and in his glorification, 'the Son of God'. Even his task as the revealer of the Father during his earthly mission has to be carried outside the limits of Jewish Messianic hopes. Jesus revealed the Father by being 'lifted up' on the Cross as 'the Son of Man', while the Jews hoped for a Christ who would remain forever (12.34).

These terms probably meant more for the syncretistic world of the Johannine Church, but they came to John from the biblical and Gospel traditions. He gave them a new sense and a singular importance as he faced a new situation in the growing Church.

---

20. J. A. T. Robinson, 'Destination and Purpose', pp. 122-123.

Chapter 6

THE HOUR OF JESUS

Throughout this book we have sought to discover what, for the Fourth Evangelist, was most significant about Jesus of Nazareth. To do this we have concentrated our attention on four names which he used to describe Jesus: the Logos, the Son of God, the Son of Man and the Christ.[1] Our enquiry has led us to see that Jesus is above all the Son of God, in the sense that he has pre-existed with his Father, and that he has entered history through an incarnation to reveal the Father in a unique fashion. Only Jesus can reveal the Father, because he comes from him. At the conclusion of his earthly mission, he will return to the Father to be glorified in his presence with the glory which had been his before the world was made (see 17.5).

There is one last feature of this Gospel, which we wish to trace out, as it helps us to follow John's thought as he takes Jesus through his life, death and resurrection: 'the hour' of Jesus. In the Synoptic Gospels 'the hour' is linked to the death of Jesus (see Mk 14.35; Lk 22.53), and we believe that this is also the case' with the Fourth Gospel. However, we are given hints throughout the Gospel that Jesus' death on the Cross is not his lowest moment, but the moment when he reveals God's love for man and a man's (Jesus') love for God in a supreme fashion. On three occasions Jesus speaks of his death

---

1. Our work is not complete. Many other aspects of the Johannine Jesus could have been considered, especially his being the second Moses, and a fuller treatment of the 'I am' sayings. Nevertheless, we feel that John's idea of Jesus is clearly presented within the limited scope which we have set ourselves. On the themes just mentioned, the reader should consult W. A. Meeks, *The Prophet-King: Moses Traditions and the Johannine Christology*, Supplements to Novum Testamentum 14 (Leiden, E. J. Brill, 1967); and P. B. Harner, *The 'I am' of the Fourth Gospel*, Facet Books, Biblical Series 26 (Philadelphia, Fortress Press, 1970).

by using a verb (*hupsoo*) which has two meanings: a 'lifting up' in a physical sense, on a stake, or a 'lifting up' in the sense of an exaltation. This tells us that the Cross of Jesus is his being 'lifted up' on his throne, so that he might reveal God, and thus give life to those who accept this revelation. The three passages make this point very clearly:[2]

> 3.14-15: 'As Moses *lifted up* the serpent in the wilderness, so must the Son of Man be *lifted up*, that whoever believes in him may have eternal life.'

> 8.28: 'When you have *lifted up* the Son of Man, then you will know that I am he.'

> 12.31-32: 'Now is the judgment of this world, now shall the ruler of this world be cast out; and I, when I *am lifted up* from the earth, will draw all men to myself.'

John, therefore, seems to have his own version of what happens at Calvary. It appears to be something more than the nailing of a man on a Cross.

1. *The role of the Passion in the Tradition*

Right from the beginning of the Christian mission — among both Jews and Gentiles — the followers of Jesus found themselves faced by a serious difficulty: How could this man Jesus, who was crucified, be the Messiah or the subject of a message of salvation? Such a message was: 'a stumbling-block to Jews and folly to Gentiles' (1 Cor 1.23). This scandal had to be answered, and the New Testament gives us several of these attempts. The words of Jesus which prophesy his coming passion (Mk 8.31; 9.30-32; 10.32-34 parrs) show that it happened because Jesus said it would. Another explanation is found in the use of the Suffering Servant hymn of Is 53. It had to happen, as it was the fulfillment of Scripture. Once 'why it happened' was understood, then the primitive community began to explain 'what it meant'. Again there are several suggestions:

---

2. The English translation of the verb *hupsoo* is in italics.

- Jesus' death is regarded as a *ransom* (Gal 3.13; 4.15; 1 Cor 6.20; 7.23); his blood is the price (1 Peter 1.18-19).
- It is presented as *exemplary* of the way all Christians must go (see esp. 1 Peter 2.21-24).
- It is often presented as a *sacrifice* (see Mk 10.45; 1 Tim 2.16). It is above all an expiatory sacrifice, often implied in the reference to Jesus' death as 'for our sakes' (*huper hemon*).

However, it was not only important to work out a theology of the Cross in an abstract fashion. The Christian message had to be preached, and thus it was necessary to tell a connected story. The question must have been asked: 'How could Jesus have been brought to the Cross by the people who were blessed by his signs and wonders?' The question is best answered by telling the story of how it all happened. Thus, one of the first stories told as a coherent narrative was the Passion Story. As is always the case, each Evangelist tells basically the same story, but handles his material in his own way to make *his* point clear. To take one example: St Mark's Gospel is often called a Passion Story with a long introduction. Mark does not soften the blow at all. Jesus really does suffer igominy and a cruel and violent death, after hanging for three hours on the Cross. But for Mark this seems to make sense. Jesus fulfills the role of the Suffering Servant in the Markan passion account. He has suffered — but for a purpose. As Isaiah puts it:

Without beauty, without majesty (we saw him),
no looks to attract our eyes,
a thing despised and rejected by men,
a man of sorrows and familiar with suffering,
a man to make people screen their faces;
he was despised and we took no account of him.
And yet ours were the sufferings he bore,
ours the sorrows he carried.
But we, we thought of him as someone punished,
struck by God and brought low.

Yet he was pierced through for our faults,
crushed for our sins.
On him lies a punishment that brings us peace,
and through his wounds we are healed.

(Is 53.2-5).

But Mark already hints at the fulfillment of the prophecy
in his account by tearing the Temple Veil, the veil of the
Holy of Holies. The old order has passed away; the symbol
of God's abiding presence with his people is at an end;
Jesus has destroyed the temple, in the face of all the
jeering. Then the centurion, representative of the Gentile
world, a new people of God, confesses: 'Truly this man was
a Son of God' (Mk 15.39). It is only through the humiliation and agony of the Cross that Jesus is vindicated — first
in the confession of the centurion and then in the resurrection.

John's passion account makes a very different point.
There is never any stress on Jesus' suffering; throughout
Jesus is presented as the one who determines his own
destiny. He appears to be proclaimed, ironically by his
enemies, as King, even on the Cross.[3] As we mentioned
above, we have been prepared for this 'exaltation' of Jesus
upon the Cross by the continual reference throughout his
public ministry to his being 'lifted up/exalted' on the Cross,
but we are further prepared by a series of references to 'the
hour'.

2. *The Johannine theme of 'the hour'*[4]

The Gospel of John seems to be presented in the light of
the 'hour' of Jesus. This 'hour' seems to give sense to the

_____

3. See, among many books and articles written on John's
Passion story, J. C. Fenton, *The Passion According to John*
(London, SPCK, 1961).

4. Unfortunately, the most up to date and complete
study of 'the hour' is not in English. See G. Ferraro, *L' 'ora' di
Cristo nel Quarto Vangelo*, Aloisiana 10 (Rome, Herder,
1974).

whole of the life of Jesus, and at the same time to divide the Gospel into three parts. In the first part, chapters 1-10 we have a constant movement towards that 'hour', and Jesus seems almost to be attracted towards it; in the second part, chapters 11-17 the salvific meaning of this 'hour' is widely explained and unfolded. It takes place in chapters 18-20. This 'hour' of Jesus seems to point to the moment in which Jesus fulfills his mission. The difference between John and the Synoptics is that the Synoptics refer to the 'hour' only at the beginning of the Passion, while John uses it throughout Jesus' public life. According to Mark, in Gethsemane, Jesus prays that the hour might pass from him (Mk 14.35). The 'hour' in the Synoptics also refers to the Passion, but in a negative way. Jesus turns to those arresting him and says: 'Now is your hour; it is the hour of darkness . . .' (see Lk 22.53). But John does not have the term only in his Passion narrative, as he draws it back to the beginning of his Gospel, at the start of Jesus' public life (2.4). His whole public life moves towards his hour and in this way John sets up a kind of tension and anticipation as Jesus moves towards the 'hour'. He is able to create this tension by keeping his readers ignorant of the exact nature of 'the hour' throughout chs 1-10. All the reader knows is that 'the hour has not yet come'.

Jesus' first public appearance is marked by a reference to 'the hour'. At the marriage feast at Cana Jesus' mother indicates that 'they have no wine' (2.3). Jesus answers: 'O woman, what have you to do with me? My hour has not yet come' (2.4). One must understand this scene in the context of the marriage festival. This is not simply a factual reporting of a wedding ceremony which Jesus attended; we have to understand the whole scene with its imagery of the wedding banquet and its use of the wine. The words of Jesus are to be understood in the context of messianic symbols. The time of the 'fulness', the marriage feast of the Old Testament, when Israel would come to the joy of the end of time, and the Old Testament references to a banquet (see Joel 2.24; 3.18; Amos 9.13; Zech 10.7), to the overflowing of wine and abundance; this is the context within which Jesus speaks of his 'hour'. In the marriage feast of Cana we have a symbolic reference to the conferring of messianic 'goods' — the 'feast' and the 'wine'. Jesus' reply to his mother tells us that the time of the fulness of the messianic gifts has not yet come ... the fulness of the messianic moment comes about for John when Jesus 'pours out' his Spirit. For John it is in the elevation on the Cross when Jesus says: it is consummated, I've done my task, and he 'pours out', 'hands over' the Spirit, that the giving of the messianic fulness takes place (19.30). The marriage feast of Cana and its miracle are not the fulness of the Spirit — the messianic riches — but an anticipation only, a sign, of what would happen on the Cross. It does, however, begin the public manifestation of Jesus. 'This, the first of his signs, Jesus did at Cana in Galilee and manifested his glory and his disciples believed in him' (2.11). However, it is only a beginning. The revelation of the glory of God in the sign leads to belief in Jesus, but the fulness of the communication of messianic goods will come at the Cross.

There are various texts in chapters 7-8 in the context of the Feast of Tabernacles where Jesus speaks of his 'hour'. In 7.4 his 'brethren' ask Jesus to manifest himself to the world.

v. 6: 'Jesus said to them: my time is not yet come, but your time is always here ...'

References to 'time' (*kairos*) here, indirectly refer to the theme of Jesus' 'hour', which has not yet come, even though the word 'hour' (*hora*) is not used. As Jesus refers to the 'time' of his *disciples*, he cannot use the term 'hour', which applies only to *Jesus himself*. This is an indication of the importance of this theme. 'The time' of the brethren cannot possibly be called 'hour'. The time of his brethren is always here because their time is ordinary time, the time of this world, the world of every day events. There is even a hint that the time of the brethren is too attached to the time of the world in v. 7: 'The world cannot hate you, but it hates me because I testify of it that its works are evil.' The brethren do not have this special 'hour'; they can, like everyone else, go up to Jerusalem whenever they like; they have no special work to do, no task in an 'hour' which is linked to the salvation of mankind.

The 'hour' of Jesus on the other hand, is very special. It is very much measured, but measured with a yardstick that they, as yet, cannot fully understand. He has yet to come to this hour, which is a specific time in the plan of the Father, but which 'has not yet arrived'. A careful reading of v. 8 shows that there is a very subtle accentuation of the *not yet* and the *this* feast, which points to a definite future moment, a moment of *another* feast — a Paschal Feast in which the Paschal Lamb himself will be slain. On this day, and *only* on this day, will Jesus finally manifest himself to the world — it will be the moment of his death and his exaltation: his 'hour'.

Twice during the Feast of Tabernacles, Jesus, explaining to the unbelieving Jews his real purpose, mission and relationship with the Father claims to be the Son of God, which to their minds is blasphemy. They will not accept his unique union with the Godhead; so in 7.30 they try to lay hands on him, but they cannot because his 'hour had not yet come'. And in 8.20: 'but no one arrested him for his hour had not yet come.' The enemies of Jesus can do nothing against him 'because his hour had not yet come'. This context of hostility indicates that the 'hour' points to his death, but the impotency of his enemies shows that the 'hour' is totally dependent upon the will of the Father — it cannot be anticipated. Even though 'the hour has not yet come', the hostility and the attempt to lay hands upon him shows a progression from the hint of 2.4. There is now a clear indication that 'the hour' is in some way connected with the death of Jesus. We are now prepared for the second series of 'hour' sayings, in which 'the hour has come'.

In our general division of the Gospel we claimed that Jn 11-12 belonged to the first half of the Gospel, dealing with the public ministry of Jesus, but yet it introduces a new theme.[5] Jesus' death is mentioned for the first time (see 11.16) and at the end of ch. 11 the decision is made that Jesus 'should die for the nation, and not for the nation only, but to gather into one the children of God who are scattered abroad.' In ch. 12 this decision is accepted by Jesus. He is sought by the Greeks ('the children of God who are scattered abroad'), and he answers their request to see him in a discourse which runs from 12.23-33. This discourse opens with the words: 'The hour has come for the Son of Man to be glorified' (v. 23). The rest of his discourse explains what is meant by 'the hour' in this context. Especially important is v. 27 as John here takes up the words of the Synoptic Gethsemane scene, and re-fashions them for his own purposes:

v. 27: 'Now is my soul troubled.'	=	Mk 14.34: 'My soul is very sorrowful.'
v. 27: 'Save me from this hour?'	=	Mk 14.35: 'Prayed that . . . the hour might pass from him.'
v. 27: 'No, for this purpose I have come to this hour.'	=	Mk 14.41: 'The hour has come.'

The uniquely Johannine point of view is reflected in the third parallel. In Mark the hour rushes upon Jesus. In John he goes forth to meet it, because, as he explains in vv. 31-32: 'Now is the judgment of this world, now shall the ruler of this world be cast out; and I, when I am lifted up from the earth, will draw all men to myself.' Just in case the reader may have missed the point, John adds a redactional note in v. 33: 'He said this to show by what death he was to die.'

Now that the die is cast, the remaining references to 'the hour' are a further deepening of our understanding of it. Both of them announce, as in ch. 12., that the hour has come, and that it is closely linked with the glorification-revelation of God which takes place in the lifting up of

5. See above, pp. 23-24.

Jesus on the Cross. In 13.1 the Evangelist announces: 'Jesus knew that his hour had come to depart out of this world to the Father' — and then explains 'the hour' by describing it as a love for his own who were in the world 'to the end', i.e., in the most perfect manner. It is important to notice the new element which is added to the description of Jesus' 'hour' in 13.1. The hint of 2.4, more clearly expressed in chs 7-8 and made obvious in 12.23, that 'the hour' of Jesus is his being 'lifted up' on the Cross is now given a further dimension: it is 'his hour . . . to depart out of this world to the Father'. The glorification of Jesus does not *cease* with the event of the Cross. Jesus is fully glorified only in his return to his Father, and this must happen *through* the Cross. John presents the glorification of Jesus as taking place in two stages which are intimately connected: the human revelation of the supreme act of love takes place on the Cross (see 13.31), but Jesus' 'hour' does not cease there. *Through* the Cross he returns to the Father, to take up the glory which was his before the world was made (see 13.32; 17.5).[6] In all of this, the relationship between the Cross and 'the hour' remains central. This is made clearer in 17.1: 'Father, the hour has come; glorify thy Son that the Son may glorify thee.' The hour for the Son's glorification has come, and in his glorification is the Father also glorified, as the Son reveals his love to the world. Having read the Gospel, with its references to 'the hour' and 'lifting up' of the Son of Man, we know that Jesus goes to his glory on the Cross, but that in this he also glorifies the Father, as he demonstrates to the world the love which stands behind the whole plan of salvation (see especially 3.16-17; 15.13; 1 John 4.12).

The word 'hour' appears once more — at the Cross: 'He

---

6. This is a modification of the thesis of a most important study, again, unfortunately not available in English: W. Thüsing, *Die Erhöhung und Verherrlichung Jesu im Johannes-evangelium*, Neutestamentliche Abhandlung 21.1 (Munster, Aschendorff, 1970[2]).

said to his mother, "Woman, behold your son!" Then he said to the disciple: "Behold your mother!" And *from that hour* the disciple took her to his own home' (19.26-27). It would be logical to give this word a merely chronological sense here, but it appears to say more than that. At the Cross Jesus founds his Church, symbolised by the seamless garment (19.23-24), and pours out his Spirit upon it in his death (19.28-30). As E. C. Hoskyns has written of 19.26-27:

> At the time of the Lord's death a new family is brought into being. If the unity of the Church is symbolized by the seamless robe, the peculiar nature of that unity is indicated here. The Church proceeds from the sacrifice of the Son of God, and the union of the Beloved Disciple and the Mother of the Lord prefigures and foreshadows the charity of the Ecclesia of God.[7]

All of this takes place — down into our own days — because of 'the hour' of the Cross.

The hour is Jesus' supreme moment, the moment when the fulness of the messianic promise came with the giving of the Spirit and the revelation of God to all mankind. This hour consists in Jesus' death, resurrection, glorification and passing to the Father. It is not a series of events, but one 'hour', and this is indicated by John's use of one verb (*hupsoo*) to signify 'lifting up' and 'exaltation'. Jesus himself tells us, 'For this have I come' (12.27), and when he finally hands over his Spirit, from his throne on the Cross, he can announce: 'It has been consummated' (19.30).

3. *Conclusion*

In 2.4 the 'hour' was indeterminate; there was no specific mention of death, just the link with the messianic promise. In 7.6-8, 7.30 and 8.20 there was a growing clarity — 'the

---

7. E. C. Hoskyns — F. N. Davey (ed.), *The Fourth Gospel* (London, Faber and Faber, 1947), p. 530. See also R. H. Lightfoot, *St. John*, p. 317; and R. E. Brown, *John*, p. 907.

hour' meant some sort of violent encounter with his opponents. In 12.23, the death of Jesus is explicit, but another element is introduced — in this death is he glorified. This theme is then caught up and explained further in 13.1 and 17.1, as we are told that through this hour Jesus will return to his glory with the Father. Thus, from the initial enigmatic reference of 2.4 to the prayer of 17.1, the term has gradually gathered its full significance. *On* the Cross is Jesus glorified, as he reveals his Father, the God who is love (see 1 John 4.8), and *through* the hour of the Cross he returns to the glory which was his with the Father before the world was made. However, 'the hour' is not only concerned with the fate of Jesus, but also with the destiny of mankind. Because of the hour the Church exists, and continues to exist in the life given to it by Jesus, 'lifted up' on the Cross to his glory (see 19.23-30).

This survey of John's very special use of a term which he found in the tradition but refashioned for his own ends gives us an insight into the profound but simple way in which John presents the Cross, not as the moment of Jesus' humiliation, 'even unto death' (see Phil 2.7-8), but as the moment towards which his whole human life has moved. It is the exaltation which completes his 'task on earth' (17.4), closing the mission which began with God (see 1.1-2 and 3.16-17) by lifting him up from the earth (see 12.32), where he has made the Father known (see 1.18), to the glory which was his before the world was made (17.5).

Chapter 7

JESUS ACCORDING TO ST. JOHN

At the heart of the four Gospels stands Jesus, but he comes to us through these pages at two levels. There is the Jesus of history — the Son of Man who walked the roads of first century Palestine, teaching, healing and preaching the Kingdom of God. This man went to a cross, but rose from the dead. Thus far we are dealing with the life, death and resurrection of Jesus of Nazareth.[1] Then there is the Christ of faith who was fully understood after the resurrection. Only after the experience of the resurrection did the earliest Church come fully to understand the role and significance of Jesus of Nazareth, and come to true faith. Now they saw and believed that he really was the Christ, the Son of Man, the Son of God, the Word, and they began to confess their faith in him in these, and many other, terms.[2]

This book has been written because we believe that each Evangelist has something different to say about Jesus. Of course, there are all-important matters where they agree,[3] but their very important differences should not disturb us. Seen

---

1. The historical Jesus, the Son of Man, the miracles, the Kingdom of God and the resurrection are among the most discussed aspects of New Testament scholarship. We have simply affirmed what we believe can be said about Jesus of Nazareth. See C. K. Barrett, *Jesus and the Gospel Tradition* (London, SPCK, 1967).

2. Again we are glossing over a central issue in New Testament scholarship by simply claiming that there is a direct link between the historical Jesus and the Christ of faith. This is often denied. See, for an excellent discussion of this question, R. Longenecker, *The Christology of Early Jewish Christianity*, Studies in Biblical Theology, Second Series 17 (London, SCM Press, 1970).

3. A very good simple presentation of this can be found in D. Senior, *A Gospel Portrait: Jesus* (Dayton, Pflaum Publishing, 1975).

from Italy, France and Switzerland, the Matterhorn appears to be three different mountains; seen by Matthew, Mark, Luke and John, Jesus of Nazareth will naturally be portrayed in four different ways. There are several factors which played a part in the formation of these various portraits of Jesus. Each Evangelist was dependent upon the records of the teaching of Jesus and about Jesus which came to him through various sources, either oral or written. Another important influence was the situation of each Evangelist's own ecclesial community. None of us is free from the influence of our social, cultural and religious environment, and the Evangelists were no exception to this.[4] Then, of course, there was the genius of an inspired author whose own personal experience of the reality of Jesus of Nazareth must have been the strongest influence in his portraying Jesus in his own particular fashion. This little book has been an attempt to trace John's portrait of Jesus.

Like the first three Gospels, the Johannine 'good news' exists because Jesus of Nazareth existed. 'Gospels', as literary documents, give a version of the life, death and resurrection of Jesus of Nazareth. Some would claim that John's work does not attempt to present Jesus as really incarnate (e.g. E. Käsemann)[5], while others believe that Jesus' being the Logos, his Sonship, his pre-existence and his returning to the Father are but a Christian version of a myth about a Gnostic redeemer, thus telling us nothing of Jesus of Nazareth (e.g. R. Bultmann).[6] These extreme positions are taken by men of great learning and faith; thus there is always much to be learnt from their considerations. However, we are convinced that the Fourth Gospel was written because the author believed that God had revealed himself to humanity in a unique way in the words, the actions, the person and especially in the Cross of Jesus of Nazareth. These events were, to John's mind, emi-

---

4. This was the point made by the Pontifical Biblical Commission's 'Instruction on the Historical Truth of the Gospels', issued in 1964 (*Osservatore Romano*, May 14th).

5. See above, pp. 55-56.

6. See above, pp. 27-28.

nently human events which ordinary men and women, with their human senses, could perceive. There is little doubt that, whoever the *writer* may have been, the same Johannine school stands behind the Fourth Gospel and the First Letter of John, even though the situation which caused the epistle, which we consider as a later document than the Gospel, has changed.[7] The importance of the physical, human appearance of Jesus is clearly stated in the prologue to 1 John:

> 'That which was from the beginning, which we have heard, which we have seen with our eyes, which we have looked upon and touched with our hands, concerning the word of life — the life was made manifest and we saw it, and testify to it and proclaim to you the eternal life which was with the Father and was made manifest to us — that which we have seen and heard we proclaim also to you, so that you may have fellowship with us; and our fellowship is with the Father and with his Son Jesus Christ' (1 John 1.1-3).

For Jesus to be the revelation of God among men he must certainly be truly human, so that he can communicate what he hopes to reveal — especially in the enigmatic, but eminently human event of the Cross. However, these considerations do not exhaust the questions raised by the Jesus of the Fourth Gospel. How can this man claim to be the unique revelation of God among his fellow-men? As we have seen, this is the utterly *reasonable* question that 'the Jews' ask of Jesus throughout the whole Gospel. Jesus' answer is one that they cannot and will not accept, as it demands that they leap outside their own categories, to accept what he claims for himself: because he is the Son of God. They refuse to accept Jesus because they are quite content with the 'gift' which God made to them in the Law of Moses: 'We have a law, and by that law he ought to

---

7. This is a vexed question. For our position, see the clear presentation of J. L. Houlden, *A Commentary on the Johannine Epistles*, Black's New Testament Commentaries (London, A. and C. Black, 1973), pp. 1-20.

die, because he has made himself the Son of God' (19.7).[8] They will never accept that he alone can reveal God with a unique authority, because they will never accept that he is the Son of God. They also fall short of understanding Jesus because they will not accept that he comes from God, and that he was, in the beginning, 'with God' (1.1). John ends all myths about special envoys from God when he announces that, 'no one has ever seen God; the only Son, turned towards the Father, he has made him known' (1.18). Jesus' origin 'with God' gives John cause to introduce a new name for Jesus — the Logos, the very Word of God, communicating with man.

While we are very conscious of the danger of fitting the Fourth Evangelist and his thought into neat patterns, we think that the evidence of the material which we have examined points to three 'stages' in John's presentation of Jesus:

   i. Pre-existence.

  ii. Incarnation and the revelation of God among men.

 iii. The return to glory with his Father.

It seems to us that John used titles for Jesus which he took from the biblical tradition to convey these three 'stages' with considerable precision.

The title which dominates Johannine Christology is 'the Son of God'. Jesus is called the Son of God at all times, whether John is speaking about his pre-existence (1.14), his incarnate presence among men (passim, but especially 3.16-17 and 5.19-26) or his return to his glory with his Father (17.1-5). The exclusively Johannine term 'Logos' is found *only* when Jesus' pre-existence is the centre of interest (1.1-2). We are told in 1.14 that the Logos became flesh, but he is then called 'the only Son', and the Logos title never again appears. Scholars claim that this limited use of the title 'Logos' is evidence for the theory of a separate existence and later

---

8. In fact, they violate the Law in convicting Jesus, yet enigmatically 'fulfill' the Law (the Scriptures) by 'lifting him up' (see 19.28-30). See, on this, the work of S. Pancaro, *The Law in the Fourth Gospel*, pp. 319-363.

insertion of a Logos-hymn. This may be so, but we would suggest that there was more to it. John was, of course, conditioned by the sources which he used, but his careful limitation of the title 'Logos' to the Prologue may have been *his* decision. The fact that the Gospel never again hints at it may well be the deliberate work of the Evangelist, as he had *his own* idea of what 'Logos' meant when he applied it to Jesus of Nazareth. It is not sufficient for John to refer to the incarnate Logos as 'the Son of God'. Never does one hear of the crucifixion of a Son of God. Thus John singles out another title from the tradition which had always been closely associated with the sufferings of Jesus: the Son of Man. This title is reserved for Jesus' role as the revelation of God in Jesus' human presence — especially in the eminently human experience of being 'lifted up' on a cross.

These appear to be the major categories which John has used to present his portrait of Jesus.[9] As we have seen, he was also anxious to present Jesus as 'the Christ', but not the Messiah who could be determined by current messianic hopes. The Johannine Messiah breaks the bounds of the limitations which Jewish hopes wished to impose upon him because his being Messiah consisted in his being, above all, the Son of God.

If all that we have argued in the foregoing pages is true, then the 'stages' of the Johannine Jesus — along with the corresponding titles which seem to describe these "stages" — can be indicated in the following fashion:

	Son of God	
Logos	Son of Man	
Pre-existence	Incarnation-revelation	Return to Father

---

9. It should be noticed, however, that they are not the *only* categories. See above, p. 101, note 1.

A final word must be said about the incomplete nature of this book. We have concentrated our attention on the Jesus of the Fourth Gospel, but what you have just read is not the whole story. The Fourth Gospel does much more than portray Jesus. It is written that we might be led to belief in the God whom Jesus reveals to us, and that we may thus come to eternal life. In other words, this Gospel is not only about Jesus of Nazareth, but also about the salvation which he has made possible for us. Both are intimately linked. It has not been the scope of these pages to show how Johannine Christology determines Johannine Soteriology (from the Greek word, *soter*, meaning 'saviour'). That could be the subject of another book. However, the intimate link between them has been repeatedly hinted at throughout this work. If Jesus is the unique revealer and the revelation of the Father as his Son, the Logos and the Son of Man (Christology), we can only be saved by an uncompromising commitment, in faith, to that revelation (Soteriology). Jesus can be called the Way, the Truth and the Light (Christology) because only in him can we find Life (Soteriology). John himself has made this clear for us as he unites Christology with Soteriology when, to conclude his Gospel, he tells his readers why he wrote it:

'These things are written that you may believe that Jesus is the Christ, the Son of God, and that believing you may have life in his name' (20.31).

FURTHER READING

There are a large number of books currently available on John, and the following list is by no means complete. However, it should serve as a guide to anyone who would like to read further into this Gospel.

Commentaries on the Fourth Gospel

Barrett, C. K., *The Gospel According to St John* (London, SPCK, 1978^2)

Brown, R. E., *The Gospel According to John*, The Anchor Bible 29 and 29a (New York, Doubleday, 1966-1970)

Bultmann, R., *The Gospel of John. A Commentary* (Oxford, Blackwell, 1971)

Lightfoot, R. H., *St John's Gospel. A Commentary* (Oxford, University Press, 1956)

Lindars, B., *The Gospel of John*, New Century Bible (London, Oliphants, 1972)

Marsh, J., *The Gospel of St John*, Pelican New Testament Commentaries (Harmondsworth, Penguin, 1968)

Schnackenburg, R., *The Gospel According to St John*, Vol 1 (London, Burns & Oates/Herder & Herder, 1968)

Selected Studies on John's Background and Theology

Barrett, C. K., *The Gospel of John and Judaism* (London, SPCK, 1975)

Boice, J. M., *Witness and Revelation in the Gospel of John* (Exeter, Paternoster Press, 1970)

Borgen, P., *Bread from Heaven. An Exegetical Study of the Conception of Manna in the Gospel of John and Writings of Philo*, Supplements to Novum Testamentum X (Leiden, E. J. Brill, 1965)

Cadman, W. H. — Caird, G. B. (ed.), *The Open Heaven. The Revelation of God in the Johannine Sayings of Jesus* (Oxford, Blackwell, 1969)

Charlesworth, J. H. (ed.), *John and Qumran* (London, Geoffrey Chapman, 1972)

Dodd, C. H., *Historical Tradition in the Fourth Gospel* (Cambridge, University Press, 1963)

Dodd, C. H., *The Interpretation of the Fourth Gospel* (Cambridge, University Press, 1953)

Forestell, J. T., *The Word of the Cross. Salvation as Revelation in the Fourth Gospel*, Analecta Biblica 57 (Rome, Biblical Institute Press, 1974)

Harvey, A. E., *Jesus on Trial. A Study in the Fourth Gospel* (London, SPCK, 1976)

Howard, W. F., *Christianity According to St. John* (London, Duckworth, 1943)

Käsemann, E., *The Testament of Jesus* (London, SCM Press, 1968)

Kysar, R., *The Fourth Evangelist and His Gospel. An examination of contemporary scholarship* (Minneapolis, Augsburg, 1975)

Lindars, B., *Behind the Fourth Gospel*, Studies in Creative Criticism 3 (London, SPCK, 1971)

Martyn, J. L., *History and Theology in the Fourth Gospel* (New York, Harper and Row, 1968)

Meeks, W. A., *The Prophet-King. Moses Traditions and the Johannine Christology*, Supplements to Novum Testamentum XIV (Leiden, E. J. Brill, 1967)

Moloney, F. J., *The Johannine Son of Man*, Biblioteca di Scienze Religiose 14 (Rome, Libreria Ateneo Salesiano, 1978[2])

Pancaro, S., *The Law in the Fourth Gospel. The Torah and the Gospel. Moses and Jesus, Judaism and Christianity according to John*, Supplements to Novum Testamentum XLII (Leiden, E. J. Brill, 1975)

Sidebottom E. M., *The Christ of the Fourth Gospel* (London, SPCK, 1961)

INDEX